ORTHO'S All About

Wiring Basics

Meredith® Books
Des Moines, Iowa

Ortho® Books
An imprint of Meredith® Books

Ortho's All About Wiring Basics
Editor: Larry Erickson
Art Director: Tom Wegner
Copy Chief: Catherine Hamrick
Copy and Production Editor: Terri Fredrickson
Contributing Copy Editor: Martin Miller
Technical Reviewer: Ralph Selzer
Contributing Proofreaders: Kathy Eastman,
  Colleen Johnson, Margaret Smith
Contributing Illustrators: Jonathan Clark, Tony Davis,
  Ron Hildebrand, Richard Skover
Indexer: Nan Badgett
Electronic Production Coordinator: Paula Forest
Editorial and Design Assistants: Kathleen Stevens,
  Karen Schirm
Contributing Editorial Assistant: Mary Irene Swartz
Production Director: Douglas M. Johnston
Book Production Managers: Pam Kvitne,
  Marjorie J. Schenkelberg

**Additional Editorial Contributions from
  Greenleaf Publishing**
Publishing Director: Dave Toht
Associate Editor: Steve Cory
Assistant Editor: Rebecca JonMichaels
Editorial Art Director: Jean DeVaty
Design: Melanie Lawson Design
Additional Photography: Dan Stultz
Technical Consultant: Michael Clark

Meredith® Books
Editor in Chief: James D. Blume
Design Director: Matt Strelecki
Managing Editor: Gregory H. Kayko

Director, Sales & Marketing, Retail: Michael A. Peterson
Director, Sales & Marketing, Special Markets:
  Rita McMullen
Director, Sales & Marketing, Home & Garden Center
  Channel: Ray Wolf
Director, Operations: George A. Susral

Vice President, General Manager: Jamie L. Martin

Meredith Publishing Group
President, Publishing Group: Christopher M. Little
Vice President, Consumer Marketing & Development:
  Hal Oringer

Meredith Corporation
Chairman and Chief Executive Officer: William T. Kerr

Chairman of the Executive Committee: E.T. Meredith III

Photographers
(Photographers credited may retain copyright ©
  to the listed photographs.)
John North Holtorf: Cover
Dan Stultz: 4-5, 8, 9, 12, 14 (TR), 16 (TL), 18-19, 20, 23
(right), 24 (bottom), 27 (bottom), 28-29, 30 (BL), 31
(BL), 32 (TL), 32 (BR), 33 (bottom), 35 (TR), 37 (BL),
40 (TL), 43 (TR), 47 (TR), 48 (bottom), 49 (top), 50
(TL), 51 (BL), 52-53, 54 (TR), 57 (top), 57 (center), 58
(TR), 59 (bottom), 60 (TL), 64 (TL), 72 (TR), 74 (TR),
76-77, 86 (TR)

All of us at Ortho® Books are dedicated to providing you
with the information and ideas you need to enhance your
home and garden. We welcome your comments and
suggestions about this book. Write to us at:
  Meredith Corporation
  Ortho Books
  1716 Locust St.
  Des Moines, IA 50309–3023

If you would like more information on other Ortho
products, call 800-225-2883 or visit us at www.ortho.com

Note to the Readers: Due to differing conditions, tools,
and individual skills, Meredith Corporation assumes no
responsibility for any damages, injuries suffered, or losses
incurred as a result of following the information published
in this book. Before beginning any project, review the
instructions carefully, and if any doubts or questions remain,
consult local experts or authorities. Because codes and
regulations vary greatly, you always should check with
authorities to ensure that your project complies with all
applicable local codes and regulations. Always read and
observe all of the safety precautions provided by
manufacturers of any tools, equipment, or supplies,
and follow all accepted safety procedures.

YOUR ELECTRICAL SYSTEM 4

Safety First **6**
From Power Company to Your House **7**
Service Panels **8**
Household Circuits **10**

Evaluating Circuits **12**
Grounding and Polarization **13**
Home Safety **14**
Inspecting for Safety **15**

BASIC SKILLS & MATERIALS 18

Cable and Wire **20**
Boxes **21**
Switches **22**
Receptacles **24**

Stripping Wire **25**
Splicing Wire **26**
Attaching Wire to Terminals **27**

ELECTRICAL REPAIRS 28

Plugs and Cords **30**
Replacing Lamp Switches **31**
Testing and Replacing Receptacles **32**
Receptacle Wiring Combinations **34**
Testing and Replacing Switches **35**
Dimmers and Special Switches **36**
GFCI Protection **37**
Circuit Breakers and Fuses **38**
Surge Protection **40**

Replacing Ceiling Fixtures **41**
Mounting Track Lighting **42**
Repairing Fluorescent Lighting **43**
Installing Ceiling Fans **44**
Repairing Doorbells and Chimes **46**
Maintaining Thermostats **49**
Under-Cabinet Halogen Lights **50**
Low-Voltage Outdoor Lighting **51**

RUNNING NEW LINES 52

Working with Armored Cable (BX) **54**
Running Wires in Conduit and Greenfield **56**
Running Cable in Unfinished Spaces **58**
Running Cable in Attics and Basements **60**
Installing Boxes in Finished Walls **62**

Installing Ceiling Boxes **64**
Running Cable in Finished Spaces **66**
Raceway Wiring **69**
Planning New Circuits **70**
Adding Circuits **72**
Telephone and Cable Wiring **74**

ADDING NEW FIXTURES 76

Adding Receptacles **78**
Ceiling Fixture with Switch **79**
Two Fixtures on One Switch **80**
Fixtures on Separate Switches **81**
Three-Way, Power to Switch, Fixture, Switch **82**
Three-Way, Power to Fixture, Switch, Switch **83**
Three-Way, Power to Switch, Switch, Fixture **84**

Three-Way with Receptacle: Four-Way **85**
Recessed Lights **86**
Bathroom Vent Fan **88**
Whole-House Fan **89**
Attic Fan **90**
Back-to-Back Outside Box **92**
Permanent Outdoor Fixtures **93**

Index **94**

Metric Conversions **96**

Clearly marked breakers help keep repairs safe and make it easier to find problems when circuits blow. To determine what circuits each breaker serves, have one person test fixtures and outlets after you turn each circuit breaker off (or disconnect each fuse). To avoid having to shout, use your phones as an intercom system (leave a phone off the hook for a few minutes before starting or call a friend who won't mind having the line tied up while you take an electrical inventory). See pages 10–12 for information on circuits.

YOUR ELECTRICAL SYSTEM

IN THIS CHAPTER

Safety First **6**

From Power Company
to Your House **7**

Service Panels **8**

Household Circuits **10**

Evaluating Circuits **12**

Grounding and
Polarization **13**

Home Safety **14**

Inspecting for Safety **15**

Household electricity is nothing to toy with. Not only can a shock injure or even kill a person, but improper wiring also is a fire hazard. Most homeowners have a healthy respect for electricity; often they are nervous about doing any repairs or upgrades themselves. This book is designed to allay that fear. It will equip you to understand what you can do yourself or to effectively evaluate the work of a pro, if you should choose to hire the work out.

In many ways, wiring is simpler than other home repair and remodeling skills like carpentry or plumbing. Wiring involves few techniques, such as taping drywall seams or sweating copper pipe, that take years of practice to master. Although you will work more slowly than a professional electrician, the results of your work can be every bit as reliable and safe as anything installed by a pro. However, wiring must be approached cautiously and systematically. This chapter introduces your home's wiring and the techniques that allow you to work safely.

ELECTRICAL CODES

If you are replacing a fixture, switch, or receptacle, you don't need to get approval from any government office. But if you will be running new wiring and installing new circuits, you must "work to code," and you may need to have a permit and your work inspected. In some locations, certain kinds of electrical work can be done only by licensed electricians.

Codes vary from, but are all based on the National Electrical Code (NEC). These codes serve an important purpose. They ensure that installations are safe. Check with your local building department before you start projects such as those described in the chapter "Running New Lines," which begins on page 52.

SAFETY FIRST

Safety must come first every time you work on an electrical project. Don't rush; take the time to think through what you are doing. Treat electricity with the respect it deserves by observing a few simple safety rules.

SHUT OFF THE POWER: The essential first steps for nearly every project are (1) shut off the power to the circuit you're going to work on, and (2) test to *make sure* the power is shut off.

Never touch wires or energized fixtures before you kill the circuit. To disconnect the circuit, go to the service panel (*see pages 8–9*) and flip the circuit breaker off or unscrew the fuse that protects that circuit. Shut the door to the service panel, and attach a note telling people to stay away. If children can reach it, lock the panel.

Before you touch any wires, use a voltage tester, multi-tester, or simple neon tester to make sure the power is off.

Caution: Sometimes two circuits send electricity to a single box or even a single receptacle, so don't assume the power is off just because you have flipped a breaker. Test each outlet and the wires in the box.

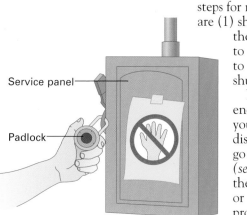

Service panel

Padlock

Neon tester

NEVER TOUCH SERVICE WIRES: You cannot shut off the two or three large wires entering the panel from the outside; they are still live even if you have shut off the switch or breakers. On the outside, keep away from the service wires, and don't work near them with a metal ladder. If you suspect a problem with the wires, call the power company.

NEVER STAND ON A WET FLOOR: Put down dry boards or a rubber mat on which to stand while you work. Also, never work with electricity if *you* are wet. Change into dry clothes before you begin.

DON'T TOUCH METAL: Radiators, metal duct work, and pipes conduct electricity. If you touch metal while also touching a live wire, the current will flow efficiently through your body, increasing the shock.

USE SAFE TOOLS: Wear safety goggles or glasses. When practical, wear gloves. Wear rubber-soled shoes; many electricians wear sneakers. Use tools with rubber- or plastic-coated handles.

TEST YOUR WORK: When your electrical work is completed, immediately turn on the power and check your work with a tester. The tester should light when a connection is made between the hot wire (usually black) and the ground wire (green or bare copper), the neutral wire (usually white), or a grounded box. It should not light when a connection is made between the neutral wire and a grounded box or a ground wire.

BE SURE: If you have the slightest doubt about any electrical work, consult with the *National Electrical Code* (available in libraries) or with your local building department. When installing new service, get a permit and follow instructions from your building inspector.

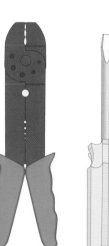

Dry boards keep you from being grounded

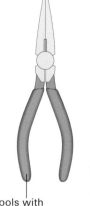

Tools with insulated handles

FROM POWER COMPANY TO YOUR HOUSE

Because it is invisible, electricity seems mysterious. But it is not complicated. Basically, electricity is the flow of minute particles of energy—electrons— through a conductor, usually a metal wire. Electricity travels in a circuit, or loop. In a home, this usually means that it flows out from the service panel through a black or colored (hot) wire to the outlet, and back to the panel through a white (neutral) wire. When the circuit is interrupted, the flow of electricity is shut off.

The path of electricity begins at the power plant, which generates high voltage electrical energy using water, coal, oil, or nuclear fuel. The power plant uses transformers to further increase voltage for transmission on high-voltage wires to substations along the line.

The substation reduces the voltage using a step-down transformer for distribution on lines running overhead or underground. For use in homes the voltage is further reduced by smaller transformers. You may see these transformers hanging on utility poles or mounted on concrete pads along streets or alleys. They make the final voltage reduction to 120 and 240 volts for use in the home.

Because electricity travels in a circuit, there must be at least two wires entering a house, one hot and one neutral. Older homes with only two wires entering can deliver only 120-volt current. Most homes now have three wires entering the house. There are two hot wires, each of which carries 120 volts. The third wire is the neutral.

If a house has underground service, the wires rise through the entrance conduit— a thick pipe—out of the ground. If the house has overhead service, the wires emerge from the transformer and enter a weatherhead on the roof or the side of a house. Here they are spliced into wires that continue down first into a meter, which measures how much electricity the house uses, and then into the service panel (*see pages 8–9*), which distributes electricity throughout the house. At the service panel, the hot wires are usually black and red and the neutral wire is usually white.

The two hot lines can be combined at the service panel to supply 240-volt current to large appliances like water heaters, kitchen ranges, or house air conditioners.

CHANGES IN VOLTAGE RATINGS

Years ago, voltage entering houses was rated at 110 and 220 volts. Since then, it has been increased to 120 and 240 volts. Older appliances and fixtures were rated at 115 volts; newer components are rated at 125 volts. You need not concern yourself about these changes. The new devices can work with old wiring, and old fixtures can operate with new wiring.

Transformer substation

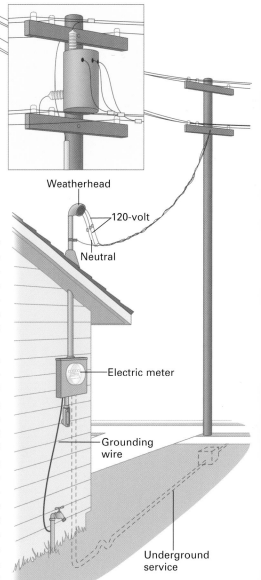

Transformer
Weatherhead
120-volt
Neutral
Electric meter
Grounding wire
Underground service

High-voltage electric energy is carried to a transformer substation where it is reduced for regional distribution. Transformers commonly seen on utility poles or set on concrete pads reduce the voltage to 120 and 240 volts for household use. Energy enters the home through wires in a weatherhead or underground conduit. The energy goes through a meter and then to the service panel inside the house.

SERVICE PANELS

Understanding your service panel is the first step toward becoming a competent and safe home electrician. It is here that electricity for your whole house is organized and distributed. And it is here that you will shut off power for almost every project or emergency.

If fuses blow or breakers trip often, one of the circuits is probably overloaded; see pages 10–12 for remedies. See pages 38–39 for information about resetting and replacing breakers and fuses.

Homes built or upgraded since the early 1960s will most likely have breaker boxes—often with plenty of room for adding new circuits.

HOW PANELS WORK

There are many types of breaker and fuse boxes, or service panels, but they all have two things in common. All service panels must be grounded *(see page 13)*, and all have a main disconnect, which allows you to shut off power to the house.

THE MAIN DISCONNECT: Power enters the breaker box or fuse box through two "hot" wires, usually black and red, and returns through a white neutral wire. These wires go immediately into a main fuse or breaker. (Older boxes may have only a black and a white wire, which is insufficient for modern electrical use; see page 15.)

To be prepared for emergencies, all adults in a house should learn how to shut off power to the whole house by flipping the main breaker or removing the main fuse. In some localities, the electrical codes require that there also be a main disconnect located outside the house. Shutting off the power at an outside disconnect will completely de-energize the service panel.

Caution: Turning off the power at the main disconnect inside the service panel will not de-energize the wires entering the box from the outside. Never touch those wires.

INSIDE THE SERVICE PANEL: Two hot bus bars (each carrying 120 volts) are connected to the main disconnect. Breakers or fuses are attached to these bars. A 120-volt breaker or fuse attaches to one hot bus bar; a 240-volt breaker or fuse attaches to both. The hot wire for each of the house's circuits is attached to the other side of the fuse or breaker. Neutral wires and green or bare copper ground wires attach to the neutral bus bar, which is electrically bonded to the panel.

GROUNDING: There should be a thick ground wire, usually bare copper but perhaps green or white insulated wire, attached to the neutral bus bar that leads out of the service panel. This is the main ground wire. It must lead deep into the ground in order to safely carry away any excess electricity *(see page 13)*. The main ground wire is sometimes connected to a cold-water pipe (which leads into the ground via other pipes), or it may lead to a rod driven at least 8 feet into the ground just outside the house.

Each individual circuit must be grounded. This is often accomplished by a green or bare copper wire attached to the neutral bar, just as the white neutral wire is. Systems that use conduit or armored cable might not have separate ground wires; the metal conduit or sheathing works as a ground wire.

BREAKERS

A circuit breaker is basically a switch that "trips" (turns off) when it senses heat. When a circuit overloads or wires short out, the circuit temperature rises and the breaker trips, shutting off power to its circuit and averting a dangerous situation. The breaker remains off until you reset it.

Some breakers will display a red tab when they've blown; others will turn partway into the OFF position. Before resetting a breaker,

---

DON'T OVERLOAD WIRES

If you have a chronically overloaded circuit, you may be tempted to install a fuse or breaker with a larger capacity. Don't. It's dangerous. A 15-amp breaker or fuse is designed to trip or blow before a 14-gauge wire gets overheated; a 20-amp fuse or breaker does the same for 12-gauge wire. Installing the wrong-sized fuse or breaker allows wires to overheat, risking a fire.

READING AN ELECTRIC METER

Electrical use is measured by a meter attached to the house. As long as an appliance is drawing current from the lines, the meter runs continuously. Some meters have counters that look like the odometer on a car, while others have four or five dials that look like clock faces. Some of these dials run clockwise and others counterclockwise.

The electric company charges its customers according to the number of kilowatt-hours (kwh) used. A kilowatt equals 1000 watts.

Read your meter once in a while to check the accuracy of the power company's readings. Write down the meter reading at the same time the company reads the meter. Read it again the following month, subtract the first reading from the second, and compare it to the bill you get for this period. If there is a significant discrepancy, contact the power company.

To read a dial meter, start with the left-hand dial and work to the right, jotting down each number.

search out and turn off or unplug the appliance that caused it to trip. Flip the breaker's switch—first all the way off, then back on. On push-button breakers, push all the way in, then release. Power will be instantly restored to the circuit.

FUSES

Older homes may have fuse boxes. These are not necessarily unsafe, but changing fuses is much more bothersome than flipping or pushing breakers. Installing a new service panel with circuit breakers in an old home may be worth the expense.

A fuse blows for the same reasons that a circuit breaker trips. Once blown, a fuse cannot be fixed; it must be replaced. So keep a supply of fuses on hand.

It may be possible in your area to buy a type of fuse that acts like a circuit breaker—instead of blowing, a small button pops out when the fuse is overloaded. However,

this device is considered unsafe by many municipal building departments.

To shut off power to a circuit, unscrew a plug fuse or remove a pullout block. Usually, the main disconnect on a fuse box is a pullout block that contains two cartridge fuses.

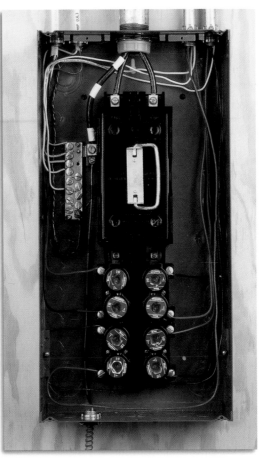

A fused, 60-amp service panel seldom meets the needs of a modern home. It's a prime candidate for an upgrade.

'RECEPTACLE' AND 'OUTLET'

Throughout this book, the word *outlet* refers to any place where electricity exits wires in order to energize an electrical component. Lights, switches, and appliances, for instance, are outlets. A *receptacle*, with slotted holes to receive plugs from lamps and appliances, is a type of outlet.

HOUSEHOLD CIRCUITS

The service panel divides electrical current into branch circuits, usually referred to as "circuits." To fully understand your home's electrical system, learn where each circuit goes and which outlets it supplies.

THREE TYPES OF CIRCUITS

The NEC divides household circuits into three categories. A well-planned system will have these three types clearly laid out.

GENERAL-PURPOSE CIRCUITS: These 120-volt circuits, usually 15- or 20-amp, supply a number of receptacles used for lighting and small appliances. Because most lights use only a small amount of power, a single circuit can supply power to quite a few.

Many electricians prefer to assign a circuit only to permanent lighting or only to receptacles. In addition, local electrical codes may demand it, although it is not an NEC requirement. It is a good idea for houses that have many permanent light fixtures.

A single receptacle is often split with each side powered by a separate circuit. This installation is especially common when one of the plugs is controlled by a switch, allowing you to switch on a floor or table lamp. (Such receptacles underline the importance of testing both pairs of openings for receiving plugs.)

SMALL-APPLIANCE CIRCUITS: These 120-volt circuits supply power to receptacles to which small appliances such as toasters and food processors will be connected. Usually, these circuits serve a reserved area—a kitchen, for example. A typical kitchen should have at least two 20-amp circuits.

INDIVIDUAL CIRCUITS: These circuits supply only one appliance, generally, those that use a lot of power. For instance, a single-use 120-volt circuit may supply a dishwasher, a trash compactor, a washing machine, or an older microwave oven. Large appliances, such as clothes dryers, electric ranges, water heaters, and large air conditioners, often require their own 240-volt circuit.

A typical 120-volt circuit serves several receptacles and/or lights; most 240-volt circuits supply only one appliance each.

MAIN
ON   ON
100
OFF   OFF

Neutral wire grounded in the earth

Receptacle   Receptacle   Receptacle   Switch

AMPS, VOLTS, AND WATTS

Think of electricity as similar to water in a plumbing system; a wire acts like a pipe to contain the flow.

■ **AMPS MEASURE CURRENT:** The volume of the current—the number of electrons flowing past a given point per second—is measured in *amperes*, or *amps*.

■ **VOLTS MEASURE PRESSURE:** The pressure under which electricity moves is measured in *volts*. Electricity arrives at household circuits at a "pressure" of 120 or 240 volts.

■ **WATTS MEASURE POWER:** Power is measured in *watts*, and you can compute wattage by multiplying amperage and volts.

For example, a standard light bulb drawing $\frac{1}{2}$ amp from a 120-volt circuit uses 60 watts of power (120 volts $\times$ 0.5 amps = 60 watts).

To calculate amps, divide watts by volts. For instance, a clothes dryer that uses 240 volts and is rated at 7,200 watts pulls 30 amps (7,200 $\div$ 240 = 30).

This means that the dryer should be protected by a 30-amp breaker, and the wire carrying current to it should be No. 10 copper, which is rated for 30 amps.

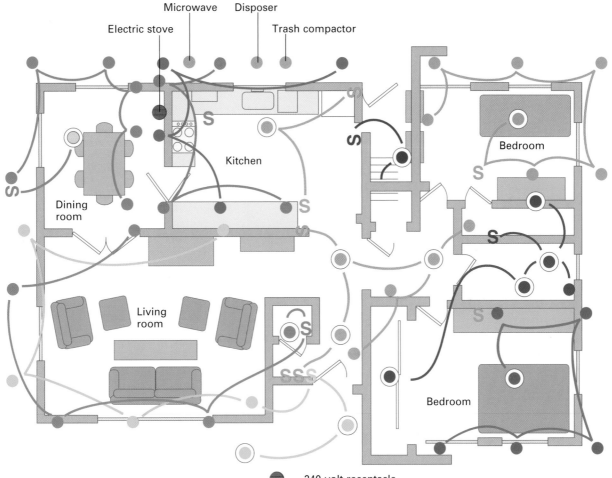

Electric stove · Microwave · Disposer · Trash compactor

Kitchen

Dining room

Living room

Bedroom

Bedroom

●	240-volt receptacle
◉	Light
●	Receptacle or direct electrical hookup
S	Single switch
SS	Double switch

AVOIDING OVERLOADS

When a circuit breaker trips or a fuse blows, it means too much current is being drawn and the wire is beginning to overheat. Frequent trips to the service panel to flip a breaker or replace a fuse are not only bothersome, they signal a dangerous condition.

RELIEVE THE LOAD: Receptacles in living rooms and bedrooms are usually used for light-duty items like lights and radios and perhaps a television, so quite a few receptacles may be hooked to a circuit in these areas.
If you plug in an air conditioner or office equipment, the circuit may become overloaded. You may be able to relieve the pressure on a circuit by moving these appliances to another circuit.

LOW-POWER APPLIANCES: Some newer appliances use less power than older models. If you have a circuit that frequently becomes overloaded, consider buying an appliance with lower amperage use. It may relieve the overload.

If steps such as these do not solve the problem, you may need to run a new circuit (*see pages 70–73*). The electrical work will actually not be too complicated; cutting holes in walls and patching afterwards will probably take most of your time.

By dividing the household area into sections fed by separate circuits, a well planned system will avoid overloads. Large appliances will be powered by their own circuits.

THE NEC

The electrical practices and procedures presented in this book are based on the *National Electrical Code,* or NEC. Sponsored by the National Fire Protection Association, the NEC establishes national minimum safety standards for electrical wiring and equipment and is updated every three years.

Most local electrical codes, whether city, county, or state, are based on the NEC, but they may vary in significant ways: They may be more stringent, or they may not be as up-to-date.

All electrical work in the home must be done according to code. Contact your building department if you are considering installing new electrical service in your home. Most building departments have regulations that are close to those of the NEC, and many will accept the NEC as an alternative.

Because it is so complex, guide books are available to help non-professionals understand the NEC.

EVALUATING CIRCUITS

In many homes, circuits are not divided rationally. There may be too many receptacles on one circuit, and only one or two on another. Some older homes, for example, were wired under early codes and have never been updated; others have been updated by homeowners without sufficient knowledge. By evaluating your circuits, you can flag problem areas and determine what improvements you need to make.

MAPPING CIRCUITS

Whether you plan to install new electrical lines or just want to understand your home's electrical system, make a detailed map or chart of your circuits. This is easier if done by two people, one at the service panel and the other testing switches, receptacles, and other outlets throughout the house (see page 4).

Draw up a floor plan of each room. Show every receptacle, switch, and fixture, as well as appliances such as an electric water heater or range that have dedicated circuits.

Turn on all the lights, and plug in and turn on several radios and lamps in different rooms. Turn off circuit number one by flipping the breaker or unscrewing the fuse, and find

Electrical devices like this mixer should have a metal tag or label stating voltage and amperage requirements, as well as wattage. If the amperage is not given, divide watts by volts. This will tell you how large the breaker or fuse should be.

IS IT OVERLOADED?

If you have a circuit that you suspect may be carrying more than it should, make sure the fixtures and devices on the circuit exceed its "safe capacity."

A circuit's safe capacity is 20 percent less than its total capacity. A 15-amp circuit has a total capacity of 1800 watts (15×120), and a safe capacity of 1440 watts. A 20-amp circuit has a total capacity of 2400 watts and a safe capacity of 1920 watts.

Figure the wattage used by all appliances, lights, and fixtures. If a device does not have a wattage rating, multiply amps times volts. Add up the wattage for all devices used by a circuit. If the total is more than the safe capacity of the circuit, plug one of the fixtures or appliances to another circuit. If you can't, you may need a new circuit.

out which outlets have been affected. Lights and radios that have turned off will help you get started. Test both plugs in each receptacle; electricians sometimes split them, putting each plug on a separate circuit. On your floor plan, write a "1" next to each outlet that is off. Do the same for all the circuits. On the service panel, jot down a summary of which outlets are protected by each circuit.

EVALUATING THE MAP: With the map in hand, evaluate your electrical distribution.

■ **ORGANIZATION:** In general, circuits should power separate areas of the house. But don't be alarmed if your wiring seems haphazard—if far-flung outlets are on the same circuit. Apparent disorganization may be confusing, but it is not necessarily unsafe, and it is not uncommon. The important thing is that no circuit is overloaded.

■ **LIGHTS ON 15-AMP CIRCUITS:** Most lights use thin wires. If a light is protected by a breaker or fuse that is 20-amps or greater, its wires can heat up dangerously before the breaker trips or the fuse blows. For this reason, lights are often put on separate 15-amp circuits. In addition, any receptacle that uses No. 14 wire must be on a 15-amp circuit; receptacles on 20-amp circuits should use heavier gauge No. 12 wire.

■ **ENOUGH RECEPTACLES:** Codes state that receptacles should be no more than 12 feet apart, and that any wall space 2 feet or wider must have at least one receptacle. This minimizes the use of extension cords, which can be hazardous if overloaded. Install a new receptacle if it eliminates an extension cord that stretches across a traffic area or that feeds a power-hungry appliance.

■ **KITCHEN RECEPTACLES:** Most overloads occur in the kitchen. Codes call for at least two 20-amp kitchen circuits. Receptacles in other areas of the house cannot be attached to these circuits. Use Ground Fault Circuit Interrupter (GFCI) receptacles near water (see page 24). A receptacle must be installed at each countertop space wider than 12 inches, and no point along the countertop can be more than 24 inches from a receptacle. Island and peninsula countertops must have a receptacle every 4 feet.

■ **BATHROOMS AND UTILITY AREAS:** Some codes call for a separate circuit serving a bathroom and another for the laundry. Hair dryers, washers, and dryers can pull a lot of amps. In addition, the proximity to water requires GFCI outlets in these areas. Garages and basements may need separate circuits as well. If you have a workshop with power tools, devote at least one 20-amp circuit to it.

GROUNDING AND POLARIZATION

Electricity seeks the quickest path back to its source or to the earth. In a properly working system that means through the wires and appliances. But a poor connection or loose wire can cause power to travel through a person's body. Grounding and polarization are features of modern electrical systems that are designed to keep electricity in the system and out of people.

POLARIZATION: Houses built since the 1920s use polarized receptacles. Polarized receptacles keep the external surfaces of appliances and fixtures on the "ground" side of the current. That way, if you touch them you won't become the ground for a "hot" surface.

GROUNDING: Most homes built since World War II have an additional protection called grounding. A third wire (or sheathing or conduit) carries wayward electricity (from a loose, or shorted, wire) safely to ground.

Each branch circuit should have a ground wire (or metal sheathing that is tightly connected at all points) leading back to the neutral bar of the service panel. From the panel, a ground cable leads to the earth. Older homes often utilize cold-water pipes for grounding, but the rising use of plastic pipes has made this practice obsolete. Construction codes today call for an outside rod firmly set into the earth to ground an electrical system.

Many building departments won't require you to upgrade an existing ungrounded system but will stipulate that all new service be grounded. If you have ungrounded service, consider having it grounded. Usually it is not practical to ground individual receptacles; entire branch circuits must be grounded.

IS IT REALLY GROUNDED?

Many do-it-yourselfers simply replace old ungrounded receptacles with new three-holed models. The resulting receptacles look grounded but are not. And even in newer homes, a grounded receptacle may not have the ground wire attached, rendering the third hole useless.

Test each of your receptacles with a receptacle analyzer (*see page 32*). It also will tell you whether the receptacle is correctly polarized.

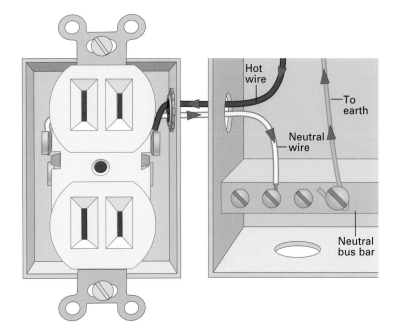

As long as it is wired correctly—with the white wire connected to the terminal with the long slot—a polarized receptacle ensures that current will not be present on the surface of a fixture. This reduces the possibility of shock during a short circuit.

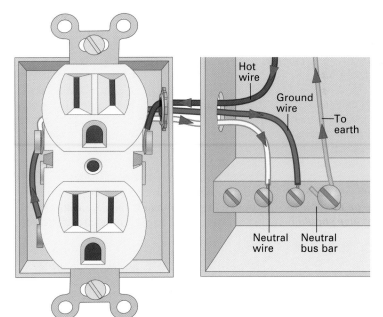

A grounded receptacle gives short-circuited electricity an unbroken path to the earth; in most cases, the power will go to the ground and not through someone's body. The third prong in a grounded plug fits into the round hole in the receptacle, which is connected through a wire or metal sheathing to the neutral bar of the service panel. The neutral bar is connected to the earth.

HOME SAFETY

Every member of your family—including children—use electricity every day. Non-conductive wall plates, grounded receptacles, wire insulation, and other protective devices make electrical service safe almost all the time. But potential sources of shock and fire may lurk undetected in even the safest-looking home. It pays to make an occasional inspection, install safety devices, and instruct everyone in proper handling of wires and appliances.

CORDS AND PLUGS: Every time you touch a cord or plug, your fingers are about $\frac{1}{16}$ inch from live electrical current. So don't take insulation for granted. Old plastic insulation can become brittle and crack; old fabric insulation can fray. Even if you can't see bare wire, replace any degraded cord immediately. Simply wrapping it with electrician's tape is not an adequate solution—the tape can easily become unwound and can cause shorts inside the insulation. And if one part of the cord is damaged, other parts may soon degrade. Replace the cord. For instructions about replacing the cord on a lamp, see pages 30–31. To replace cracked plugs, see page 30.

RECEPTACLES AND CHILDREN: If a child pokes a metal object or a finger into a receptacle, the result can be disastrous. Install protective covers on all receptacles not being

Frayed wire

Don't run a cord under a rug or carpet: Traffic can wear the insulation. Worst of all, the damage won't show until a fire starts.

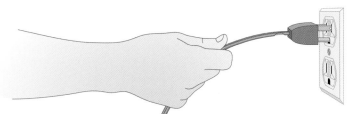

Never pull on a cord to remove it from a receptacle. The cord or the connection to the plug can be damaged.

COVER BARE BULBS

A bare bulb generates enough heat to cause fabric or paper to smolder and ignite. In closets, install a fixture that covers the bulb and position it high enough that it won't be in contact with flammables. To avoid leaving the light on while the closet door is closed, install a specialty switch on the jamb that shuts off the light when the door is closed.

used. Or install safety receptacles, which have covers that must be rotated before the plug can be inserted into them. Take measures to keep small children away from receptacles altogether.

FIRE HAZARDS: A bare light bulb quickly becomes very hot and can ignite paper or fabric that touches it. Use a bare bulb only when you are certain it will not be in contact with flammable materials.

Cords, especially those attached to older appliances, also can get hot. Check the cords on your toaster, iron, air conditioner, and similar devices. If one feels hot while in use, keep it well away from carpets and other flammable materials, or buy a newer appliance—one whose lower current requirements won't cause its cord to overheat.

INSPECTING FOR SAFETY

D on't assume that your electrical system is safe just because you haven't had a mishap. Improper or inadequate wiring may not cause a problem for decades, but it has the potential for trouble nonetheless.

Here are some of the most common wiring hazards. This list is by no means complete; if you have reason to suspect other dangers, have an electrician make an inspection.

CABLE AND WIRE HAZARDS

If you have exposed electrical cable—most likely in a basement, garage, or attic—examine it for damage. See that it is not vulnerable to bumps (are boards leaning against wiring in a shop area?) or improper use (are clothes hung from a cable?). It's easy for people to forget that the cable contains potentially dangerous electricity.

Turn off the power to the circuit and test for the presence of electricity before making any cable repairs.

EXPOSED AND LOOSE CABLE: Cable should not be stapled to the underside of a joist, where it is vulnerable. If you have such conditions, you can install new cable. Where cable runs through joists, drill holes 2 inches or more away from the underside of the joists and run the cable through it.

Wherever cable hangs loosely, use cable staples (or clamps for metal cable) to hold it tight against a framing member, the ceiling, or a wall. Fasten them every 3 feet or so, to safeguard against snags and pulls.

EXPOSED WIRE SPLICES: Wires spliced outside a box pose a fire hazard. All splices must be enclosed in an approved electrical box. Firmly attach a new box, run the cables into it using cable clamps, connect the wires with wire nuts, and install a cover on the box.

SERVICE PANEL PROBLEMS

Open the service panel door and look for signs of moisture. If you see rust, find the source of moisture and seal it with caulk.

INSUFFICIENT SERVICE: Service of less than 100 amps may be adequate if you do not use a lot of appliances. But if you blow fuses or trip breakers regularly, it is probably time for new service and a new panel.

See that the panel is not overloaded: On each bus bar, the amperage of the fuses or breakers should add up to not much more than the amperage rating of the box.

LIGHTS ON THE WRONG CIRCUITS: Check that all lights are on 15-amp circuits. Lights have lower gauge wires, which can overheat long before a 20-amp fuse or breaker blows or trips.

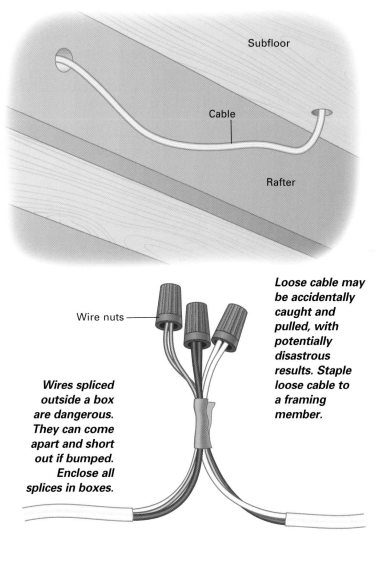

Subfloor

Cable

Rafter

Wire nuts

Wires spliced outside a box are dangerous. They can come apart and short out if bumped. Enclose all splices in boxes.

Loose cable may be accidentally caught and pulled, with potentially disastrous results. Staple loose cable to a framing member.

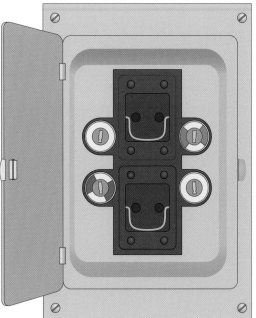

This 60-amp service panel was not intended to handle all the electrical appliances a modern household requires. For your safety and to avoid changing fuses, replace it with a breaker box.

INSPECTING FOR SAFETY
continued

Replace a cracked receptacle immediately; it is prone to shorting out.

UNSAFE RECEPTACLES AND SWITCHES

Use a receptacle analyzer (*see page 32*) to test each receptacle for grounding and polarization. If a switch or receptacle is cracked or damaged in any way, replace it. Shut off power and test to make sure the power is off before probing or making repairs. Remove cover plates and inspect switches and receptacles for cracks and improper wiring.

TWO WIRES ON A TERMINAL: It is against most codes to have two wires connected to a single terminal. If you discover terminals with two wires attached, remove them, connect them to a short length of wire called a pigtail (*see below* and *page 34*), and fasten the pigtail to the terminal. (Some electricians strip insulation from the middle of a wire so a single wire can enter and leave a terminal without being cut; this is permissible with most codes.)

TOO MUCH WIRE EXPOSED: If too much insulation has been stripped from a wire attached to a terminal or a wire nut, the exposed wire could touch another or a metal box and cause a short circuit. Loosen the connection, remove the wire, and cut off all the stripped wire. Then strip ¾ inch of insulation, bend the wire, and reinstall it (*see page 25*). If you simply cut part of the exposed wire and rebend it, the wire might break.

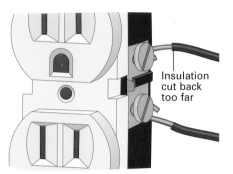

Insulation cut back too far

Cut back and restrip wires that have too much bare wire showing; they may touch other wires or the side of a metal box and short out.

UNPOLARIZED CONNECTIONS: Even if you do not have a receptacle analyzer, you can see whether a receptacle is polarized by checking the wires. The white wire should be connected to the silver-colored terminal (the one that connects to the longer hole), and the black or colored wire should be hooked to the brass-colored terminal.

HAZARDS IN BOXES

To check the wiring in boxes, first shut off the power, remove the cover plate, and test to make sure the power is off. Unscrew and pull out the receptacle or switch; in a junction box, pull out the mass of wires.

DEBRIS: Even a small amount of sawdust, dirt, or drywall crumbs can cause a short circuit. Vacuum out any debris.

CROWDING: When wires are forced into a box that is too small, wire nuts can come loose and insulation can be damaged. Codes

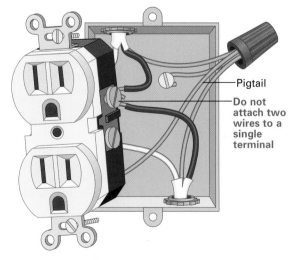

Pigtail

Do not attach two wires to a single terminal

Codes prohibit attaching two wires to a single terminal, because the terminal screw may not hold both of them securely.

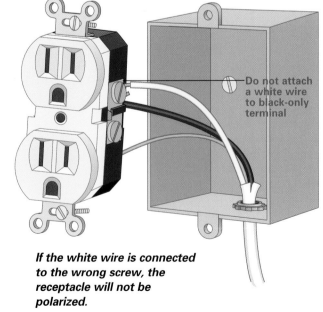

Do not attach a white wire to black-only terminal

If the white wire is connected to the wrong screw, the receptacle will not be polarized.

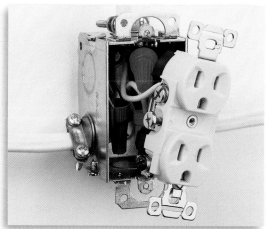

Don't cram too many wires into a box—you run the risk of causing a short. Turn off the power, disconnect the wires, and install a larger box.

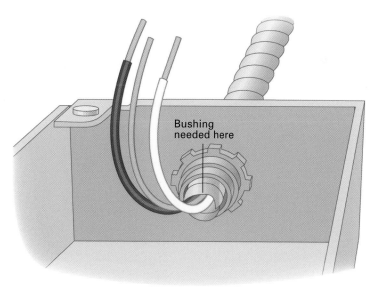

limit the number of wires allowed in a box. This number varies according to the thickness of the wire and the size of the box. For instance, a No. 14 wire requires 2 cubic inches of space, and a No. 12 wire needs 2.25 cubic inches. But you don't need a code book and a calculator to tell when a box has become overcrowded. If a tangle of wires is crammed into a box, untangle and disconnect them, keeping careful track of which wire goes where. Install a larger box (perhaps a deeper one that fits in the same wall or ceiling hole), and reconnect the wires.

MISSING CABLE CLAMP: Switch and junction boxes are fitted with knockout holes for cable entry. If a cable is poked through and not clamped at the knockout hole in a metal box, the sheathing and insulation can easily become damaged. Plastic boxes usually do not need clamps, as long as the cable is stapled to a framing member near the box.

DAMAGED INSULATION: Even a small nick in insulation can lead to a dangerous short. Pay special attention to the point where wires enter the box; this is often where older insulation becomes frayed. If damage occurs only in one spot, wrap it with electrician's

tape. If the insulation has failed at several points, chances are it also is damaged in places you cannot see; replace the entire length of these wires.

MISSING BUSHING: Armored (or BX) cable has sharp edges that can quickly take a bite out of wire insulation. Special plastic sleeves called bushings, usually red, wrap around the wires and slip into the sheathing to protect insulation (*see page 54*). You can install these without disconnecting any wires.

RECESSED BOX: The front edge of a box should be nearly flush with the wall or ceiling surface. If the box is set back from the surface—especially wood paneling—you have a fire hazard. Move the box out, or attach an extender to the box.

Without a protective bushing, wire insulation is easily damaged by the sharp edges of armored cable.

A recessed box, especially if it is set back behind a wood-paneled wall, poses a fire hazard.

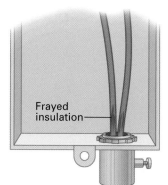

Frayed insulation

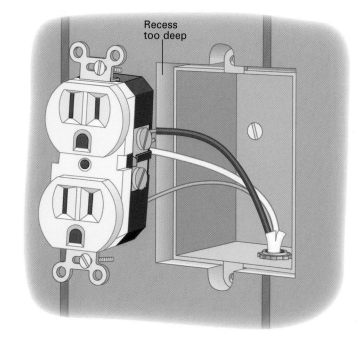

Recess too deep

A bucket outfitted with a tool apron easily holds all the electrical and carpentry tools you need. The apron keeps tools organized, and those that are too large for it are easily retrievable from the bucket.

KEEP IT CLEAN

All remodeling work, including wiring, creates dust and mess. Cutting into a wall will produce wallboard dust or plaster particles that travel all over the house if not cleaned up quickly. To ease cleanup, take a minute to spread a drop cloth on the floor. For a large project, buy a roll of construction paper (rosin paper) and some masking tape to cover the floor.

Wire strippers

Lineman's pliers

Long-nosed pliers

Drywall saw

4-way screwdriver

Basic Skills and MATERIALS

IN THIS CHAPTER

Cable and Wire **20**
Boxes **21**
Switches **22**
Receptacles **24**
Stripping Wire **25**
Splicing Wire **26**
Attaching Wire to Terminals **27**

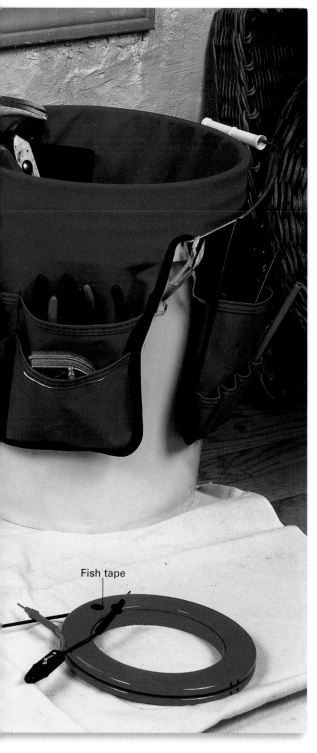

Fish tape

Home electrical projects call for only a few specialized tools. Purchase quality items that will serve you well and last a long time. **Lineman's pliers** work much better than other pliers for twisting wires together, and you also can cut wires with them. Several types of wire strippers are available: An **adjustable wire stripper** is not impressive-looking, but once set to the right wire gauge, you won't have to search for the correct hole every time you strip wire. A combination tool has a series of holes for different sizes of wire (see page 25). Use **fish tape** to run wires through conduit or to pull cable through walls and ceilings; it works much better than the old unbent coat hanger. Use a **drywall saw** to cut holes for boxes; a reciprocating saw is useful if you have a lot of cable to run in unfinished space. These are the basics; you'll find other tools explained in the book as they are used.

Tools for running cable include a cable ripper for nonmetallic cable (page 25), a BX cutter for stripping armored cable (page 54), and a tubing cutter for cutting conduit (page 56).

Also purchase testing equipment. An inexpensive neon tester (pages 31–33) tells you whether power is on and fixtures are functioning. Use a continuity tester (page 35) to check wiring when the power is shut off or an appliance is not hooked up. Use a receptacle analyzer to test receptacles for grounding and polarization (pages 32–33). A volt/amp meter (page 47) indicates how much power is present and tests appliances, motors, and transformers.

CABLE AND WIRE

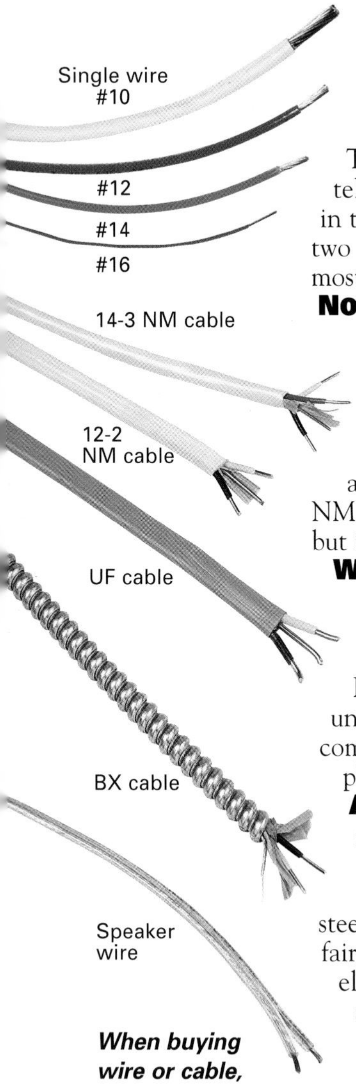

Choose the wire and cable that are correct for the job. The wrong cable or wire size could create a fire hazard and would have to be replaced in order to pass inspection. Here are your options.

SELECTING CABLE

A cable is two or more insulated wires wrapped in sheathing. Most cables carry two or three wires, plus a ground wire. The numbers printed on the sheathing tell you how many wires of which size are in the cable. For instance, "14-2" indicates two No. 14 wires (plus a ground wire in most cases).

NONMETALLIC: Nonmetallic (NM) sheathed cable is the most commonly used cable for residential wiring. It contains two or three insulated wires, plus a bare copper wire, all in a paper wrapping and encased with moisture- and flame-resistant plastic sheathings. NM cable is easy to use and inexpensive; but its sheathing is easily damaged.

WATERPROOF: Type UF (underground feeder) nonmetallic cable has the wires encapsulated in solid PVC sheathing. Use it wherever wiring might get wet. In some localities you can bury UF cable underground by itself, while other communities require that it be run through plastic conduit.

ARMORED: Armored, or BX, cable has insulated wires running in a flexible metal jacket. The newer, aluminum-clad BX is lighter and easier to use than the older steel-clad type. Because the armor provides a fair amount of protection to the wires, local electrical codes often permit it in areas that are semiexposed, such as basements or inside cabinets. BX may contain a green-insulated ground wire. In many systems, however, the sheathing itself acts as the ground (see page 13).

CONDUIT: Commercial and some residential wiring often use conduit instead of cable. Conduit, often called "thin-wall," is metal or plastic pipe through which wires are run. It is more expensive, but very safe.

WIRE

Wire in cable that runs in walls is made of a solid strand of metal; wire in appliance and extension cords is made of many thin strands wound together. Cord wire can be bent many times without breaking.

Single wire #10

#12

#14

#16

14-3 NM cable

12-2 NM cable

UF cable

BX cable

Speaker wire

When buying wire or cable, you need to consider the type (single insulated, sheathed, or armored), wire size, and number of wires in the cable. Above are common cables used in home remodeling.

INSULATION: Wires made prior to the mid-1960s may have rubber or cloth insulation, both of which become brittle and crack over time. Newer wires are coated with vinyl, which is more durable and lasts longer.

TYPE OF METAL: Most wire is made of copper. But for a few years in the late 1960s, some wire was made of aluminum. If your cable is stamped with "AL" and your wires are silver-colored, you have aluminum wire. Take care: Dissimilar metals in contact with one another cause corrosion. If an aluminum wire is connected to a brass or copper screw, it could come loose after a few years. Use only receptacles and switches specifically designed for use with aluminum wire.

COLOR CODING: Some nonprofessionals don't pay attention to wire insulation color—and that's dangerous. Wire colors give you specific information about each wire's purpose. A white wire is neutral, carrying power back to the service panel. A black wire is hot, carrying power out to the receptacle or appliance. A bare or green-insulated wire is used as a ground wire. A red wire is hot. Red, blue, and other colors indicate hot wires. Sometimes electricians alter the color scheme for different circuits. A white wire that has been painted black or wrapped with black tape indicates that it is being used as a hot wire (see examples on pages 80–82).

WIRE SIZE: The thicker the wire, the more current (amperage) it can carry without overheating.

The same applies to cords. Light-duty household extension cords generally are thick enough to handle a total of only 1,600 watts, or about 13½ amps. For heavy-duty appliances, buy a heavier gauge extension cord. Some appliances have limits on the length of even heavy duty extension cords.

Use the chart below to determine which wire to use with which circuit.

THE RIGHT WIRE FOR THE AMPERAGE

Wire Size	Amps
No. 14	15
No. 12	20
No. 10	30
No. 8	40

BOXES

Any electrical connection—to a switch, to a receptacle, or even a splice to other wires—must take place inside a box. All boxes must be accessible; never cover an electrical box with drywall or woodwork. (Some appliances and fixtures have their own built-in boxes.)

CHOOSING THE RIGHT BOX: If a box is too small, the wires will be cramped, creating a potentially dangerous situation (*see page 17*). Codes are very specific about how many wires of which size can go in a box. The two most common examples: Standard 2½-inch-deep switch boxes can handle a switch or receptacle plus six No. 14 wires or five No. 12 wires. A 4-inch-square junction box that is 1½ inches deep safely holds 10 No. 14 wires or nine No. 12 wires. If you think a box may be overcrowded, buy a deeper box, or an extension for a junction box.

SWITCH BOXES: Also called "utility boxes" or "handy boxes," these hold switches or receptacles. A single switch box is 2 inches by 3 inches. Some metal switch boxes are "gangable;" you can remove one side of each box and join them together to form boxes for two or more devices.

CEILING BOXES: Sometimes called "outlet boxes," these are octagonal or round. Use them for ceiling fixtures.

JUNCTION BOXES: These are square. Use them at every junction where you need to splice wires; leave them exposed and cover them with flat "blank plates" if they are used for junctions only. To install a switch or receptacle in them, use a switch or receptacle cover.

NEW-WORK BOXES: When installing wiring in an unfinished space (with exposed framing and no drywall or plaster), use new-work boxes for quick and easy installation. Most are designed to install ½ inch out from the framing. That means they will be flush with the wall once wallboard is installed. Some are equipped with nails so you can

simply position them on a framing member and whack them in place with a hammer. Others have nailing brackets that hold the box at a precise location.

OLD-WORK BOXES: It's more difficult to install a box in a wall with a finished surface. Make it easier by using a box fit that does minimal damage to the surrounding area. Some boxes grab the drywall with flanges when you tighten a screw; others use plastic "ears" that swing out and move forward as you tighten screws (*see page 64*).

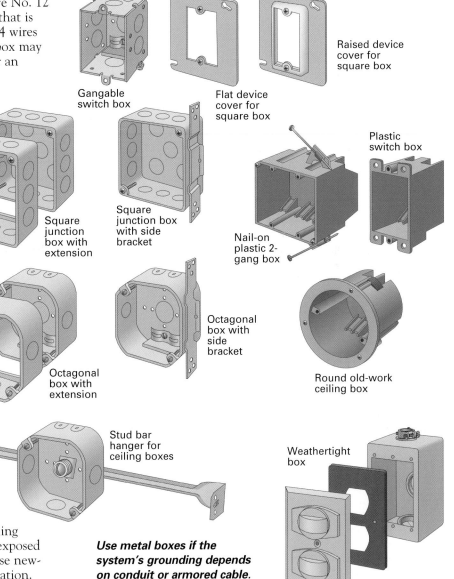

Gangable switch box

Flat device cover for square box

Raised device cover for square box

Square junction box with extension

Square junction box with side bracket

Nail-on plastic 2-gang box

Plastic switch box

Octagonal box with extension

Octagonal box with side bracket

Round old-work ceiling box

Stud bar hanger for ceiling boxes

Weathertight box

Use metal boxes if the system's grounding depends on conduit or armored cable. Plastic boxes are the usual choice when working with NM cable with a ground wire.

SWITCHES

Pictured here are some of the most popular switches. A trip to a home center will reveal many others.

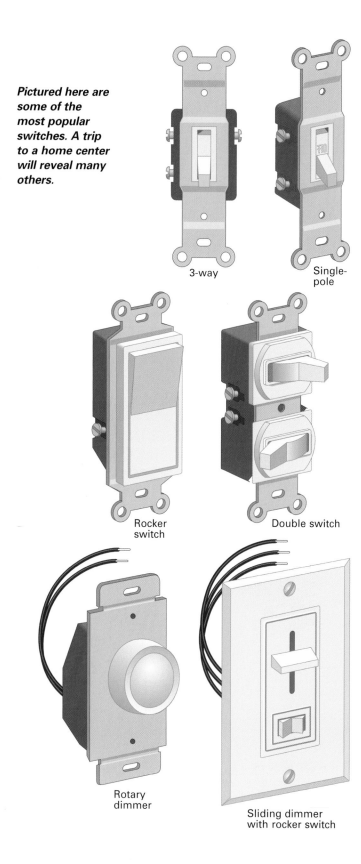

3-way

Single-pole

Rocker switch

Double switch

Rotary dimmer

Sliding dimmer with rocker switch

At its most basic, a switch opens and closes a wiring loop to shut off and turn on a light, fixture, or appliance. However, there are many variations on this basic theme.

THE BASICS

First, make a decorating decision: Ivory, brown, or white are the color options. Then choose whether you want standard toggle switches that you flip up and down, or more expensive rocker switches, which you control by pressing one side or the other.

GROUNDING: Some switches have a green grounding terminal. Most codes do not require that switches be grounded, though some codes require grounded switches in damp areas like bathrooms and basements.

SINGLE-POLE: Chances are, four out of five of your switches will be this type. A single pole switch is a "two-way" switch—it has two settings (on and off) and two terminals.

THREE-WAY AND FOUR-WAY: Use two three-way switches to control a light from two different locations (*see pages 82–84*). To add more switches controlling the same light, use four-way switches (*see page 85*). A three-way switch has three terminals, and a four-way switch has four terminals, but neither has ON and OFF printed on the toggle.

DOUBLE SWITCH: When adding a circuit for a new switched light, spare yourself the trouble of installing a new box by using a double switch, one for the existing circuit and the other for the new one. It fits into the same space as a single switch. Make sure there is enough room in the box for the extra wires (*see page 21*).

DIMMERS: A dimmer allows you to increase or decrease the intensity of the light—and to turn it on and off. Do not use a dimmer to control a fan or other motor; without a consistent voltage, the motor will burn out in short order. For a fluorescent fixture, you will need a special, fairly expensive dimmer switch. You can purchase three-way dimmer switches as well.

A rotary dimmer is the least expensive. One type turns the light on and off with a push; the other type turns the light off when you rotate the knob all the way counterclockwise. A sliding dimmer with a rocker switch allows you to turn a light on and off at the brightness of your choice. Toggle dimmers look just like regular two-way switches.

SPECIAL-USE SWITCHES

Here are a few of the many switches designed
to meet specific needs. For instructions on
installing them, see page 36.

PILOT-LIGHT: This switch has a bulb that
glows when the switch is on. Use it when the
fixture or light is not visible from the switch
location, such as an attic fan or garage light.

TIMER: There are two basic types of timer
switches. One has a dial control that tells a
fixture to turn off or on after a certain time
interval. Another has a dial that you can set
so that a light will turn on and off at the same
time every day.

PROGRAMMABLE: This rather expensive
switch gives you many more options than a
timer switch. It is much like a small computer
that you can program to turn a fixture on and
off at certain times of the week. When you're
out of town, it can give the impression that
your house is occupied.

MOTION-SENSOR: This comes equipped
with an infrared "eye" that gazes over a wide
area to detect motion and turn on the light.
Better models can be adjusted for sensitivity.

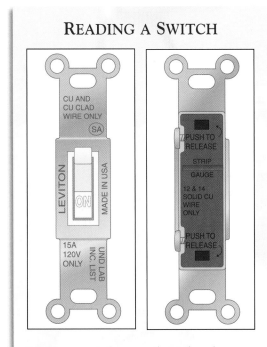

READING A SWITCH

Examine a switch to see that it has the
correct amperage rating and that it is
approved by a testing agency such as the
Underwriters Laboratories (UL). The back
tells what size wire it accepts. The strip
gauge shows how much insulation to remove.

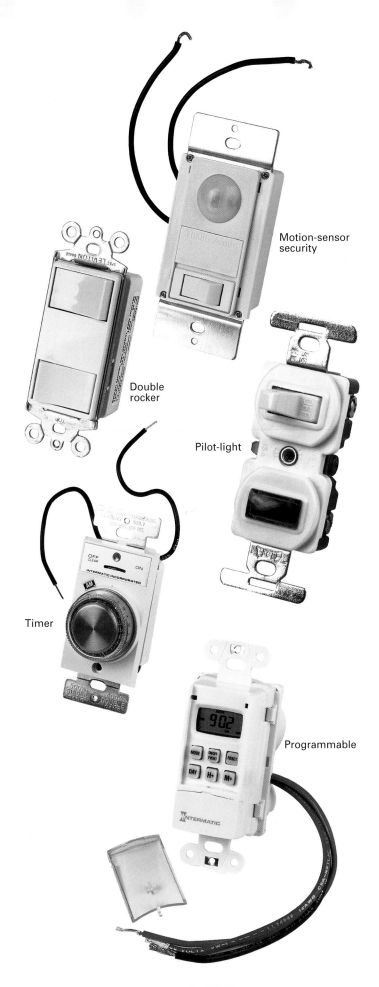

Motion-sensor
security

Double
rocker

Pilot-light

Timer

Programmable

RECEPTACLES

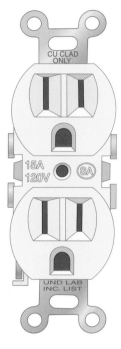
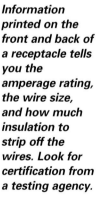

Most receptacles sold today are grounded, but don't replace an ungrounded receptacle with a grounded one unless you also change the wiring *(see page 13)*. Not all receptacles are equal in quality. The bin of inexpensive receptacles you may find at your hardware store or home center will not be as durable as models that cost a bit more. It is worth the extra expense to have receptacles that resist cracking.

125-VOLT RECEPTACLES:
The most common of these have two outlets. Many styles have a metal tab that connects the two. Cut it to wire each outlet to a separate circuit. To ensure grounding and polarization, connect the white wire to the outlet's long slot, the black wire to the short slot, and the ground wire to the round hole for the grounding tang.

Match the receptacle to the circuit wiring. Use a 20-amp receptacle with No. 12 wires and a 20-amp fuse or circuit breaker; use a 15-amp receptacle with No. 14 wire and a 15-amp fuse or circuit breaker.

A switch-receptacle takes up the same space as a standard switch. You can hook it up so the switch controls the receptacle, or so the receptacle is always hot and the switch controls a fixture *(see page 34)*.

GFCI receptacles offer extra protection by detecting even tiny shorts (caused by human contact) and shutting off the power. Install them wherever a receptacle might get wet *(see page 37)*. If an appliance needs to snug up against a wall and the plug would be in the way, use a recessed receptacle.

250-VOLT RECEPTACLES: Appliances that call for 250-volt receptacles have specific amperage requirements. Choose a receptacle that corresponds to the appliance amperage requirements and make sure the holes match the appliance plug. Plugs vary in shape according to whether the unit pulls 15, 20, 30, or 50 amps. Choose a floor-mounted or wall-mounted device to fit your installation.

While other configurations are available, these are the receptacle types used in most homes.

Information printed on the front and back of a receptacle tells you the amperage rating, the wire size, and how much insulation to strip off the wires. Look for certification from a testing agency.

20-amp

Switch/receptacle

GFCI

Recessed, or clock-hanger

250-volt 20-amp, single-grounded

125/250-volt, 50-amp floor-mounted

125/250-volt, 50-amp wall-mounted

STRIPPING WIRE

Stripping wire is something you will do over and over again in the course of electrical work, so invest in quality tools and take the time to hone your technique. With practice, it will take you only a few seconds to strip just the right amount of insulation from a wire. Pay careful attention; make sure you do not accidentally cut any needed insulation.

REMOVE SHEATHING: Strip away cable sheathing without damaging the wires inside. For NM cable, use a cable ripper, an inexpensive tool that digs just deep enough to cut through the sheathing. Slide 8 inches or so of cable into the ripper. Squeeze so the cutter pokes through the middle of the cable, and pull to slit a line back to the end of the cable. Now you can pull the sheathing off the wires and cut it back with a cutting pliers or a knife.

   If you don't have a cable ripper, carefully use a utility knife. Cut down the middle so the blade hits the bare grounding wire but not the insulation of the hot or neutral wire.

   To remove sheathing from armored cable (BX), see page 55.

STRIP THE WIRE: To attach a wire to a switch or a receptacle terminal, first strip off the right amount of insulation—usually ¾ inch. (Check the back of a switch or receptacle to confirm the right amount. It is stamped with a stripping gauge. Use these gauges until you have gained a natural sense for the correct amount of insulation to remove.) To strip wires for splicing, remove about an inch of insulation.

   It is important to cut the insulation but not the wire; even a shallow nick will weaken it. Combination tools and some models of wire strippers have a series of grooves; fit the wire into the groove that corresponds to the wire gauge you are stripping. To use a pair of adjustable strippers, set the depth so it just cuts through the insulation. Squeeze the tool, twist to cut all the way through, then pull off the insulation.

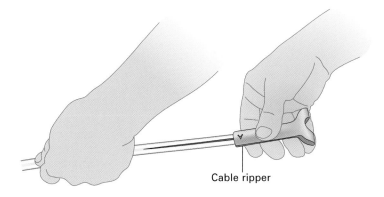

Cable ripper

1. For NM cable, use a cable ripper to cut a line in the sheathing, then cut the sheathing away with a knife.

2. To use a wire stripper or combination tool, place the wire in the correct groove and squeeze.

3. Rotate the tool while squeezing, until the insulation is cut through. Then pull off the insulation.

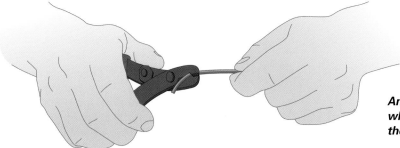

An adjustable wire stripper is handy when you're stripping many wires of the same gauge.

SPLICING WIRE

Make all wire splices inside an electrical box. The box must remain accessible for repairs—never cover it over with drywall. If there is any possibility of confusion about which wires go where, label them as you run them, using indelible markers. Or, gently twist together wires that all go to a certain device; that way, when it's time to do the finish work, the connections will be obvious.

TWISTING WIRES

Like stripping, splicing seems straightforward; but it is easy to get it wrong. If wires are not twisted tightly enough, they can come loose; if twisted too hard, a wire can break or a wire nut can crack. Professional electricians quickly twist wires into a tight coil that looks as if it were made in a factory. That kind of splice ensures a long life and a solid electrical connection. With practice, you can make the same kinds of splices.

Twist solid wires together by grabbing both with the pliers and rotating.

Lineman's pliers

To join a stranded cord wire to a solid wire, wrap the cord wire around the solid wire, and fold the solid wire over.

To twist two solid or stranded wires together, strip an inch of insulation from each. Hold them next to each other—parallel, not crossed. Using lineman's pliers (other pliers do not work nearly as well), grab the ends of both wires and twist clockwise about three revolutions. Both wires should turn an equal amount; do not twist one wire around the other. Don't overtwist, or a wire may break. Screw a wire nut onto them.

When installing lights, you often need to twist together a stranded wire and a solid wire. To do this, strip off more insulation—about 1½ inches. Wrap the stranded wire tightly around the solid wire. Then fold the solid wire over and squeeze firmly with pliers. The wires are ready for a wire nut.

USING WIRE NUTS

Electricians once wrapped splices with tape, but codes now require wire nuts. Use them to cap wires you have twisted together. With care, you can use the nuts to do the twisting.

Choose a wire nut that can house all the wires you want to splice. Usually, red wire nuts can handle two to four No. 12 wires or two to five No. 14 wires; yellow nuts house two to three No. 12 wires or two to four No. 14 wires; and orange nuts can take two No. 12 wires or two to four No. 14 wires. Check the packaging to be sure.

Do not strip too much insulation or bare wire will be exposed below the nut. One inch is fine. Poke both wires into the nut and twist for several revolutions, until the nut is tight. Check that both wires are tightly captured.

To be safe, wrap the bottom of a wire nut with electrician's tape (see page 33).

A special wire nut for connecting bare ground wires has a hole through its top. Poke the ground wires through the hole and twist.

1. To join wires together using a wire nut, hold the wire ends tightly together and insert them both.

2. Twist the wire nut clockwise onto the wires.

3. Check that no bare wire is showing. If it is, twist off the wire nut and trim back the wires. Test the splice by pulling on each wire. They should be firmly anchored in the wire nut.

ATTACHING WIRE TO TERMINALS

A proper terminal connection is tight, with all of the wire captured under the terminal screw. There should be very little stripped wire exposed beyond the screw. With practice, you can make professional-quality connections like these.

STRIP AND TURN THE WIRE ENDS: When installing a receptacle in an unwired box, strip the sheathing back to where the cable enters, leaving the wires long enough so they can easily fold back into the box and stay clear of the switch or receptacle. Use the gauge on the back of the terminal to determine how much insulation to strip—usually about ¾ inch.

Strip the wire and, with a pair of long-nosed pliers, grab the tip of the stripped wire and form a U-turn loop.

ATTACH TO THE TERMINAL: Twist the wire or position the terminal so that the loop can wrap clockwise around the screw and so it lays flat against the side of the terminal. A black or colored wire goes to the brass terminal; the white wire goes to the silver-colored terminal.

If necessary, loosen the terminal screw to make room for the wire. Slip the wire loop under the screw head and pull the loop back until it fits tight. Fasten the screw firmly, but do not overtighten.

Wrap the perimeter of the receptacle or back of the switch with electrician's tape, so all bare wires and all terminal screws are covered. This extra precaution may prevent a short circuit if a wire comes loose in the box.

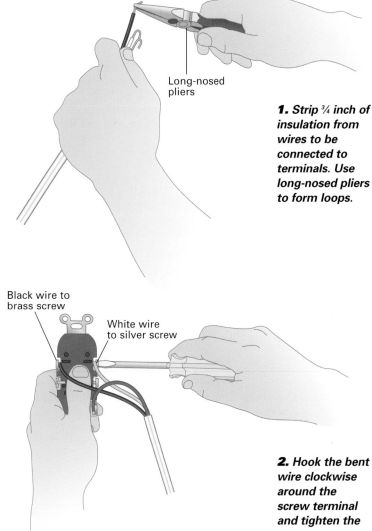

Long-nosed pliers

1. Strip ¾ inch of insulation from wires to be connected to terminals. Use long-nosed pliers to form loops.

Black wire to brass screw

White wire to silver screw

2. Hook the bent wire clockwise around the screw terminal and tighten the screw.

USING CONNECTION HOLES

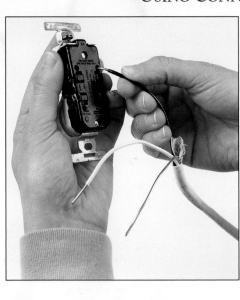

Many switches and receptacles have poke-in connection holes in the back. These allow for easy connections. Instead of twisting a loop and fastening with a screw, simply poke the stripped wire end into the hole. To free a wire for removal, jab a small screwdriver into a slot near the hole.

Before using this method, be sure you have the right-sized wire. Many devices work well with No. 12 wire but will not capture No. 14 wire tightly. Also, be sure to insert the black or colored wire into the hole near the brass terminal, and the white wire into the hole near the silver-colored terminal. Many professionals refuse to use these holes; they believe that connections made this way are not as reliable or secure as those made with terminal screws.

Incandescent lamps vary greatly in appearance, but all have similar wiring, with a cord running through the lamp body and ending at a socket. Their uniform construction makes most lamps relatively easy to repair.

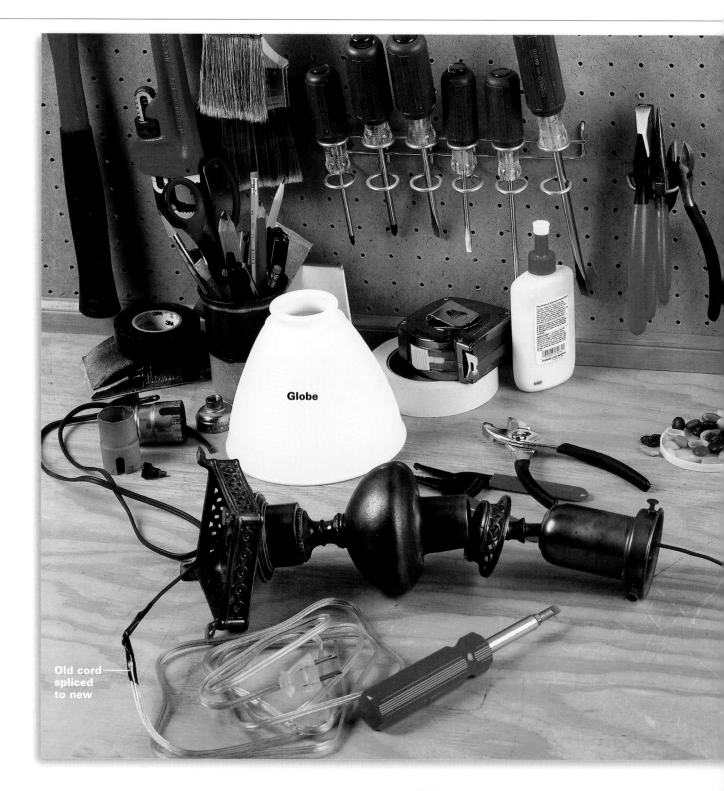

Globe

Old cord spliced to new

ELECTRICAL REPAIRS

Outer shell

Insulating sleeve

Socket cap

Old socket

New socket

This chapter is about repair work. It will show you how to fix a cord or troubleshoot a doorbell—as well as how to install switches and receptacles in existing boxes and wire new fixtures such as back lighting and ceiling fans. None of this work requires a permit since there are no new circuits, cables, or electrical boxes.

For example, lamp wiring is simple. Generally two things may require that you rewire a lamp: The cord can be damaged by misuse or age, or the socket (which usually contains the switch) can go bad. If you need to replace one, you may as well replace the other, since they've aged together.

If the bulb flickers, try this simple fix. *Unplug the lamp.* Remove the bulb. Reach down into the socket with a slot screwdriver and gently pull up on the metal tab that makes an electrical connection to the bulb base; it may have flattened out. Plug in the lamp and test.

If that doesn't solve the problem, *unplug the lamp* and take it apart. Remove the bulb and shade. You may need to remove a harp, the wire that holds the shade, by squeezing it and pulling up. Pull out the socket and remove its outer shell by pressing where it says "push" and lifting up; you may need to pry with a screwdriver. Pull out the cardboard insulating sleeve. Examine the cord and the socket for damage. To replace the cord, tape the new cord to the old and pull it through. Tie an underwriter's knot (see page 30) in the cord just below the socket.

IN THIS CHAPTER

Plugs and Cords **30**

Replacing Lamp and Overhead Light Switches **31**

Testing and Replacing Receptacles **32**

Receptacle Wiring Combinations **34**

Testing and Replacing Switches **35**

Dimmers and Special Switches **36**

GFCI Protection **37**

Circuit Breakers and Fuses **38**

Surge Protection **40**

Replacing Ceiling Fixtures **41**

Mounting Track Lighting **42**

Repairing Fluorescent Lighting **43**

Installing Ceiling Fans **44**

Repairing Doorbells and Chimes **46**

Maintaining Thermostats **49**

Under-Cabinet Halogen Lights **50**

Low-Voltage Outdoor Lighting **51**

PLUGS AND CORDS

For safety's sake, replace a plug whenever it is cracked or its prongs are loose; replace a cord if its insulation is damaged in any way. Electricity is only a fraction of an inch from your fingers when you handle a cord or a plug, and replacements cost very little.

INSTALLING A NEW ROUND PLUG: Purchase a replacement plug designed for your cord and appliance. Cut the cord off the old plug. Strip 3 inches of sheathing and ¾ inch of insulation from each cord wire. Slip the cord

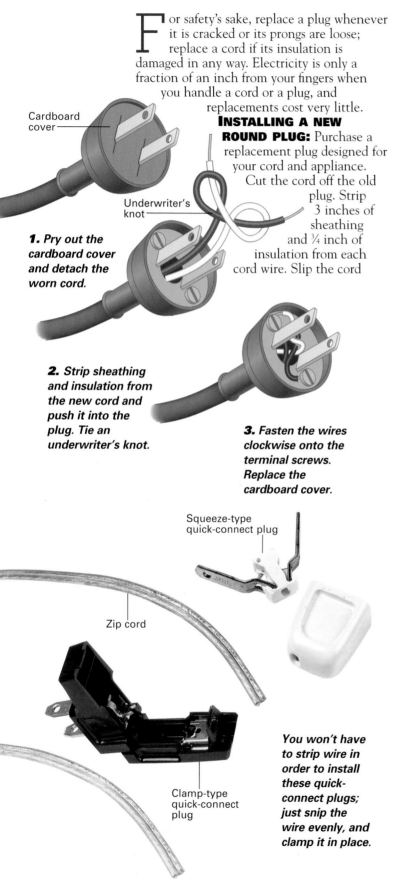

Cardboard cover

Underwriter's knot

1. Pry out the cardboard cover and detach the worn cord.

2. Strip sheathing and insulation from the new cord and push it into the plug. Tie an underwriter's knot.

3. Fasten the wires clockwise onto the terminal screws. Replace the cardboard cover.

Squeeze-type quick-connect plug

Zip cord

Clamp-type quick-connect plug

You won't have to strip wire in order to install these quick-connect plugs; just snip the wire evenly, and clamp it in place.

through the hole in the back of the plug. Tie the black wires in an underwriter's knot (*see left*). (If you have three wires and a two-pronged plug, you have the wrong plug.) Pull the cord back so that only wires, and no sheathing, are exposed. Use long-nosed pliers to turn the stripped wire ends clockwise around the terminals (black to brass and white to silver). Tighten the screws down on the wire ends, and slip on the cardboard cover.

QUICK-CONNECT PLUGS: If the fixture used "zip" cord (two-wire, thin and flat), buy a plug designed for easy connection. There are several types available; most do not require you to strip wires.

To install a squeeze-type quick-connect plug, disassemble the two pieces. Poke the cord through the hole in the body, and into the hole in the prong assembly. Squeeze the prongs together—sharp points on the prongs make the electrical connections. Then slide the prong assembly into the body. When it snaps in place, the repair is finished.

A clamp-type quick-connect plug may be even easier. Pry open the plug, set the wire in the slot so it lays flat, and close the cover. Push down hard until it snaps.

POLARIZED PLUGS: If one prong of your old plug is wider than the other, you have a polarized plug (*see page 13*). Replace it with another polarized plug. Before you remove the old plug, make sure you know which wire goes to which prong and wire the new plug the same way. Often, the neutral wire will have a ridge running all along its length; this wire goes to the wider prong.

GROUNDING: Don't remove the third, round grounding prong; it is an important safety feature. (Appliances and tools that are "double-insulated" provide protection from shock without a grounding prong.)

CHOOSING CORD: Never install a new cord that has thinner wires than the old cord. Light-duty zip cord can be easily "unzipped" to separate the two wires. Use it for lamps and radios. Speaker cord has clean insulation and is commonly used where it will be visible— for instance, running through a chandelier's chain. If you use speaker cord, be sure to use a heavy-gauge stock.

Cord with 16-gauge wire is acceptable for appliances pulling 15 amps or less; 12-gauge wire will handle up to 20 amps. For an extension cord, add up the total amperage of all the appliances that will use it at one time (*see page 20*), and choose a gauge that will handle the total amperage.

REPLACING LAMP AND OVERHEAD LIGHT SWITCHES

If a lamp or overhead light fails to come on, first twist the bulb clockwise to check that it is screwed in tightly. If it still doesn't light, remove the bulb to see if it is burned out. Often you can hear a rattle when you shake a burned-out bulb, but test by putting in a new bulb even if you hear nothing.

If the bulb is not the culprit, check the wiring and the switch. For troubleshooting a wall switch, see pages 34–35. If your light has a pull-chain switch or a small toggle switch mounted on it, follow these steps:

TEST THE WIRING: Shut off the power at the service panel for an overhead fixture; unplug the lamp. Disassemble it so that you can get at the wiring. Unscrew the wire nuts connecting the switch leads to the cord or cable. Don't untwist the wires. Position the bare wire ends so that they cannot contact each other or any metal surface.

Restore power or plug back in, and touch the two probes of a neon tester to the two bare connections. If the tester glows, power is flowing to the switch. The switch needs to be replaced. If the tester does not glow, shut off power and examine the wiring leading to the fixture or lamp. A connection may be loose.

REPLACE A SWITCH: Shut off the power or unplug the lamp. Untwist the switch leads from the wiring. Unscrew the mounting nut, and remove the switch. Install a new switch to match, and connect its leads to the wiring with wire nuts.

Some inexpensive pull-chain lights have a built-in switch that cannot be replaced.

This type of switch is typically short-lived. If you have a fixture-mounted switch that is used often, consider running wiring in the wall and installing a wall switch; it will give you less trouble in the long run.

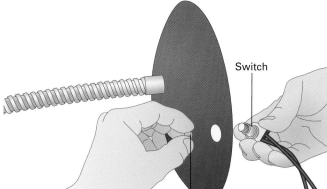

Switch leads

Neon tester

Once you've checked that the bulb works, use a neon tester to make sure power is getting to the switch.

IN-LINE SWITCHES

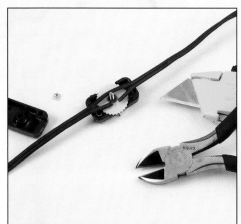

A feed-through cord switch, also called an in-line switch, makes it easy to add a switch to a lamp or appliance that does not have one. (For example, many computer peripherals do not have switches.) You do not have to strip wires to install this type of switch. Pull the plug and cut out a 1-inch section of one wire (either wire will do). Disassemble the switch, place the cord in the slot, reassemble, and tighten the screw. Work the switch by rotating the wheel.

Switch

Mounting nut

It's impractical to try to repair a fixture-mounted switch. Replacement switches are inexpensive, and take only a minute or two to install. Simply unplug the lamp and remove the felt (if any) that covers the bottom of the base. Unscrew the mounting nut to release the switch; attach the new switch leads to the cord with wire nuts.

TESTING AND REPLACING RECEPTACLES

Receptacles are inexpensive and easy to replace, so install new ones if yours fail to energize appliances, or even if you don't like the color or style. Make sure you choose a receptacle to suit the amperage and grounding configuration of your circuit (*see page 24*).

Pen-type mini-voltmeter

TEST FOR POWER

Check the service panel to see that the receptacle's power is on (*see pages 8–9*). Test both outlets (top and bottom) by inserting the probe of a pen-type mini-voltmeter into each of the slots. It will light up and buzz if power is present. Or insert the probes of a neon tester or a voltmeter into both slots of each outlet. If the tester doesn't respond in both outlets, test further.

Shut off power to the circuit at the service panel. Remove the receptacle cover plate, unscrew the two screws holding the receptacle to the box, and gently pull out the receptacle.

Turn the power back on, and test for current by touching one tester probe to the brass screw and the other first to the silver-colored screw, then to the box, if it is metal.

If the tester glows, turn off the power and examine all the wire ends carefully. One may be broken inside the insulation or may not be connected to the receptacle. If the wires are in good shape, the problem is with the receptacle; replace it.

If power is not present, the problem could be a faulty breaker, blown fuse, or defective wiring in a receptacle up the line (*see page 34*). If all other receptacles work, test the wires for power, starting at the service panel and moving outward. If you cannot find the trouble spot, call in an electrician.

IS IT GROUNDED AND POLARIZED?

A receptacle may seem to work just fine even though it has its polarity reversed or is ungrounded (*see page 13*). Check for these dangers with a receptacle analyzer (*see box below*), or use a neon tester or voltmeter.

With the power on, insert one prong of the tester into the short (hot) slot and the other into the grounding hole. If the receptacle is grounded and correctly polarized, the tester will glow.

If you do not have a receptacle analyzer (right), use a neon tester. Stick one probe into the short slot and one into the ground hole. If the tester glows, the receptacle is grounded and polarized.

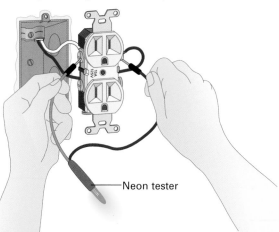

Neon tester

Test the wires to see whether power is entering the receptacle. If power is present and the receptacle does not work, replace it.

USING A RECEPTACLE ANALYZER

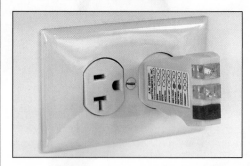

Armed with this tool, you can test all the receptacles in your house in an hour or so. Unplug most of the cords and turn off switches connected to the receptacle's circuit. Plug the analyzer in. Glowing lights will tell you if the receptacle is ungrounded or not polarized and will identify the wires that you need to rearrange in order to solve the problem.

If it doesn't glow, insert one probe into the long (neutral) hole and one into the grounding hole. If it glows, the receptacle is not correctly polarized; shut off power, remove it, and reverse the black and white wires. If the tester does not glow with one prong in the grounding hole and the other in either slot, the receptacle is not grounded.

REPLACING RECEPTACLES

Check the service panel for the breaker size in the circuit. Install a receptacle with an amperage rating that matches the breaker. Warning: A 15-amp receptacle hooked to a 20-amp circuit could overheat dangerously.

Shut off the power. Pull the receptacle out. Loosen the terminal screws, and pull out the wires. If any wire ends appear damaged, cut them back, strip, and bend into a loop (see page 27). Attach wires to the new receptacle in the same configuration as the old (after testing for polarization, as discussed above). Wrap the receptacle with electrician's tape to cover all exposed wire and terminal screws. Connect the receptacle to the box with the two screws.

Neutral wire

Hot wire

Wrap with electrician's tape

Ground wire

To replace a receptacle, shut off the power, remove the cover plate and receptacle. Unscrew and pull out the wires, inspect them for damage, and reattach them to a new receptacle. Wrap with electrician's tape.

INSTALLING A GROUNDED REPLACEMENT

If you have an old ungrounded receptacle with only two slots and no grounding hole, it may actually be grounded. To test, remove the cover plate. Insert one prong into the short slot and touch the other to the metal box. If it glows, the box is grounded. You can install a grounded receptacle even though there is no grounding wire. (Attach a wire from the ground to the box, if the outlet has one.) Metal sheathing or conduit will provide the ground.

If the tester glows with one prong in the long slot and the other touching the box or the cover plate's screw, the box is grounded but the receptacle is not polarized. Install a grounded receptacle, and wire it correctly (see above). If the tester does not glow during any of these tests, the box is not grounded. Do not install a grounded receptacle.

RECEPTACLE WIRING COMBINATIONS

Often, there's more to wiring a receptacle than hooking two wires to two terminals. Different wiring configurations are used for different tasks. Your home probably has some of these wiring arrangements. Familiarize yourself with them so you can be aware of trouble spots and to install new circuits. To run cable and install new receptacles of your own, see pages 52–73.

MIDDLE-OF-THE-RUN WIRING: When a receptacle is in the middle of the run, the wiring runs through the box and out toward other outlets. Some older homes have middle-of-the-run receptacles connected to four wires so the electricity flows through the receptacle terminals before leaving the box. In this case, if one receptacle is damaged, it can shut off

power to all other receptacles. To replace a damaged receptacle with 4-wire wiring, connect it with short lengths of wire called pigtails.

SWITCHED RECEPTACLES: A receptacle controlled by a wall switch usually has both a power cable and a cable running to the switch. When the break-off tab is removed, the receptacle can be "split" so that one outlet is controlled by a switch and the other is always hot—a useful arrangement if you want to turn on a single lamp with a wall switch.

SWITCH AND RECEPTACLE: These can be wired so that the switch controls both a light and the outlet. Or the outlet can be wired so it remains hot even when the switch is off.

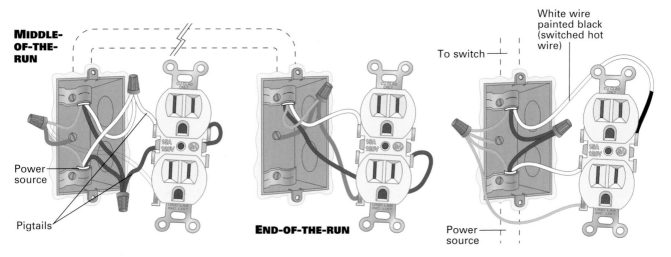

If cable enters and leaves the box, the receptacle is in the middle of a run. Use pigtails to attach the receptacle. If cable enters but doesn't leave the box, it's at the end of the run.

This receptacle is switched so that both outlets are controlled by a wall switch.

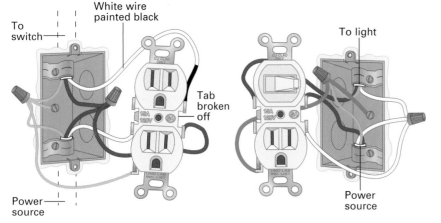

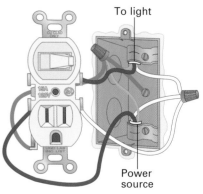

This receptacle has one outlet switched and one always hot.

Wire a switch/receptacle so the switch turns the outlet and a light on and off.

A switch/receptacle can also be wired so the outlet is always hot.

TESTING AND REPLACING SWITCHES

S witches are cheap and easy to install. Don't try to fix a switch that is cracked, flops loosely, or fails to turn a light on and off. Replace it instead. To install a dimmer, three-way, motion-sensor, or other special-use switch, see page 36.

TEST A DOUBLE-POLE SWITCH: Shut off power to the circuit. Remove the cover plate and mounting screws, and gently pull the switch out. Restore power. With the switch turned to OFF, touch the probes of a neon tester or a voltmeter to each of the terminals. If the tester glows (or indicates power), power is entering the switch. Turn the switch on, and test again. If the tester glows with the switch on, the switch is defective; replace it.

Or, test with a continuity tester. Shut off power to the circuit. Remove the cover plate, pull out the switch, and disconnect the wires. Attach the tester's alligator clip to one terminal, and touch the probe to the other. The tester should glow when the switch is turned on and stop glowing when the switch is off. If not, replace the switch.

TEST A THREE-WAY SWITCH: Shut off the power. Remove the switch completely, disconnecting all wires. Attach a continuity tester's clip to the common terminal—the one with the darker screw. The tester should glow when the probe touches one of the other terminals, but not the other one. Flip the switch; the tester should glow when the probe touches the other terminal only. If the switch fails either of these tests, replace it.

REPLACE A SWITCH: Shut off power to the circuit. Remove the cover plate and the screws holding the switch to the box. Pull the switch out, loosen the terminal screws, and remove the wires. Warning: For a three-way switch, it is essential that you mark each wire so that you can match each wire to the correct terminal of the new switch.

Inspect the wire ends. If they are nicked, snip them off, strip insulation, and form new loops using long-nosed pliers (see page 27). If the switch is wired using connector holes in the back, don't try to pull the wires out; instead, snip them off, strip insulation, and bend new loops.

Connect the wires to the terminal, and tighten the screws. Wrap electrician's tape around the switch body to cover all wire ends and terminals. Push the switch and wires back in the box, and attach the switch to the box using screws.

Before you tighten the screws, place the cover plate over the switch to make sure the switch is level and the cover plate is positioned where you want it. Replace the cover plate and test the switch.

Continuity tester

With a continuity tester, you can test devices while the electricity is off. Never use one when power is present; one jolt of 120-volt current will destroy it.

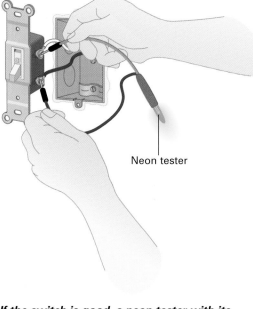

Neon tester

If the switch is good, a neon tester with its probes touching each terminal will glow when the switch is off, and not glow when the switch is on.

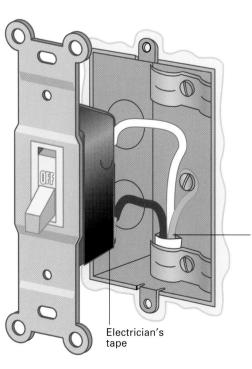

Ground wire

Electrician's tape

After making firm connections to both terminals, wrap the switch body with electrician's tape. Then, carefully tuck the wires into the box and mount the switch with screws.

DIMMERS AND SPECIAL SWITCHES

Modify your electrical service in a hurry by installing a switch that performs a special duty, such as dimming, turning on and off at specified times, or turning on when there is motion in the area. See page 23 for other options.

Usually, switches do not have to be grounded unless they are subject to damp conditions, as in a bathroom. However, it won't hurt to connect a switch's green ground wire to a copper ground wire. If your switch does not have a grounding wire or terminal, just make sure all the ground wires are connected in the box.

Wire a dimmer by connecting its leads to house wires with wire nuts.

DIMMER: Be sure your dimmer can handle the light fixture it is assigned to. If a dimmer is overloaded, it will make a buzzing sound and eventually fail.

Inexpensive dimmers are rated to 600 watts only, not enough for a chandelier. Heavy-duty dimmers go all the way up to 2,000 watts.

Dimmers have leads rather than terminals. Connect them to the wires with wire nuts (*see page 26*). On a single-pole dimmer, hook black to black and red to white. For a three-way dimmer, label the wires before removing the old dimmer so you will be sure which leads go to which wires. Begin wiring with the "common" lead. The common terminal on a standard three-way switch has a dark-colored screw; on a dimmer, the common lead is marked on the switch body (*see pages 82–84*).

MOTION-SENSOR AND TIMERS: These special-purpose switches are also wired with wire nuts. There are two possible wiring

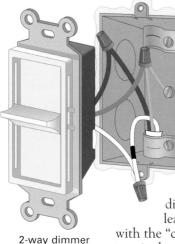

2-way dimmer

When replacing a three-way switch with a three-way dimmer, mark the "common" lead attached to the black screw head on the switch. Connect it to the common lead of the dimmer.

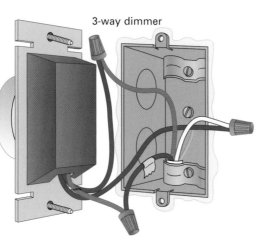

3-way dimmer

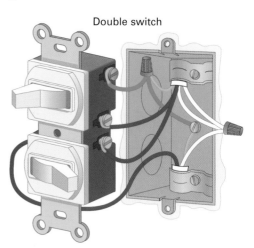

Motion-sensor

Wire a motion-sensor or other special-use switch as you would a standard two-way (see page 79), but attach leads rather than hooking wires to terminals.

schemes: If power travels through the switch on its way to the fixture or light, tie the house's white wires together, and tie the black wires as shown for the motion-sensor switch *above*. If power goes to the fixture first, paint the end of the white wire leading to the light black, and wire as shown for the two-way dimmer *at left* (*see page 79*).

DOUBLE SWITCH: A double switch has its hot terminals connected with a tab and neutral terminals separated. It is easiest to wire with power coming into the switch, rather than with power entering the lights first. Connect the house's hot wire to the terminal on the side with a connecting tab. Connect the lights' black wires to the other terminals, and hook all the white wires together in the box.

Double switch

To connect a double switch, attach the house's hot wire to the single terminal, and the hot wires leading to the fixtures to the other terminals.

GFCI PROTECTION

A ground fault circuit interrupter (GFCI) provides protection in addition to that provided by grounding *(see page 13)*. A GFCI detects even tiny current leaks and shuts off power within milliseconds. Small current leaks are a potential danger only if a person will be extremely well grounded, for instance, someone who is barefooted and standing on a wet floor. That is why GFCI receptacles are required by most codes for bathrooms and for all receptacles within a few feet of a sink.

Plug-in GFCI

PLUG-IN GFCI: This is by far the easiest to use: simply plug it into any receptacle or extension cord, and whatever tool or appliance you plug in to the device will be protected. Keep one in your tool box, and use it whenever you are working with power tools outdoors, especially when the weather is wet.

RECEPTACLE GFCI: If there is room in the box, replace a standard receptacle with a GFCI *(see page 33 for general instructions on replacing a receptacle)*. By installing a GFCI in the middle of the run, all the receptacles down the line will disconnect power if shorted by human contact. Hook the "Load" leads to the lines going out, and the "Line" leads to incoming power.

You may not want GFCI protection on certain other receptacles. For instance, you would not want a digital clock or a computer to shut down whenever the GFCI for another receptacle trips. In this case, purchase a GFCI that does not have "Line" leads, and hook it up with pigtails as you would a standard receptacle *(see page 34)*.

GFCI CIRCUIT BREAKER: This will protect all the outlets on the circuit. It essentially offers the same protection as a breaker but with much greater sensitivity to interruption. It is wired and snapped into place like any other circuit breaker. See page 38 for installation instructions.

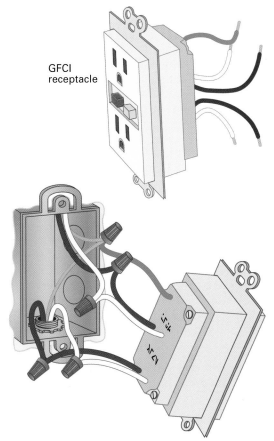

GFCI receptacle

Replace a standard receptacle with a GFCI. Instead of screw terminals, it may have leads that attach to household wiring with wire nuts.

To wire a GFCI receptacle in the middle of the run, hook the "Line" leads to incoming power, and "Load" leads to wires that go to other receptacles. If you are installing at the end of a line, cap off the "Load" leads.

BOX EXTENDER

GFCIs are much bulkier than standard receptacles, and often won't fit comfortably in a standard box. Cramming it in creates a dangerous situation, and is forbidden by code *(see page 17)*. The best solution is to remove the box and replace it with a deeper one, but this is a lot of work and usually means tearing into a wall. There's another solution: Use a raceway wiring box *(see page 69)* to extend the box outward. Throw away the portion of the raceway box that you do not use, and purchase extra-long mounting screws to attach it to the wall box.

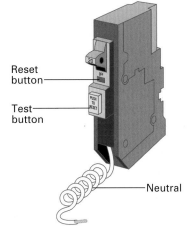

GFCI circuit breaker

Reset button

Test button

Neutral

You can use a GFCI breaker to protect an entire circuit from shorts and potential shocks.

CIRCUIT BREAKERS AND FUSES

A service panel is the control center of your home's electrical system, and it may seem forbidding and dangerous. But if you take a few simple safety precautions, working on it is no more complicated than replacing fixtures, switches, or receptacles. In fact, in many ways it is simpler, because all the elements are within easy reach. See pages 8–9 to gain a general understanding of service panels.

SAFETY

Always remember two primary safety rules for working with breakers and fuses:
■ When you need to touch wires or the hot bus bar, shut off power to the box by flipping the main breaker or pulling the main fuse.
■ Never touch the wires that come from the power company that attach to the main shutoff.

HOW BREAKERS WORK

A circuit breaker turns itself off when it senses too much heat, thereby preventing wiring from overheating.

ON, OFF, AND TRIPPED: Get to know your breakers so you can identify a tripped one at a glance. There are several types. One type flips partway off when it trips; to reset it, flip the tab off first, then on. Another type has a red tab that either becomes visible or protrudes when the breaker has tripped; press in and release to reset.

SIZE AND AMPERAGE RATINGS: Most breakers are about ¾ inch wide and are controlled by a single tab; these are 125-volt, and are rated for 15 or 20 amps. A "skinny" breaker is half the width but does the same job as its thicker siblings. Use a skinny breaker to install a new circuit when there is no more room in the panel. A double breaker has a bar connecting the two toggles, and it protects 250-volt circuits.

REPLACING A BREAKER: Like a wall switch, a breaker can become defective and need replacing. If all the outlets on a circuit are off and the breaker won't turn them on, the breaker likely needs replacing. Purchase an exact duplicate; a home center will have a chart telling you which new breakers can replace which old breakers.

Replacing a breaker is surprisingly easy. Shut off the main breaker; this will turn off power to your whole house, so you may need

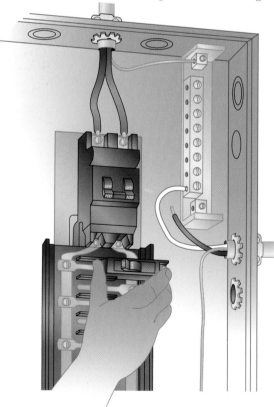

To replace a circuit breaker, shut off power to the service panel by flipping the main breaker. Loosen the screw that captures the black or colored wire, and pull the wire out. In most cases, you can then simply pull the breaker out. Push the new one into place and reattach the wire.

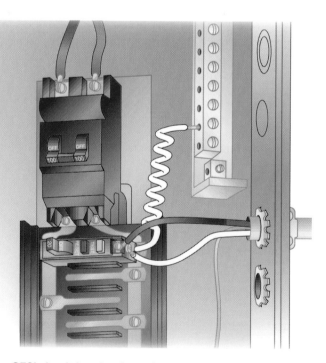

Snap a GFCI circuit breaker into place as you would a standard breaker. Connect the circuit's black or colored wire to one terminal, attach the white wire to the other terminal, and attach the GFCI's coiled white wire to the panel's neutral bar.

a flashlight. Disconnect the black wire from the breaker by loosening a screw and pulling the wire. Pull the breaker out; you may have to first yank in one direction, then the other. Push and snap the new breaker into place, and reattach the hot wire.

To install a GFCI circuit breaker, follow the same procedure. However, also remove the breaker's white wire from the neutral bar by loosening a screw and pulling the wire. Attach the hot wire to one of the breaker's terminals, and the white wire to the other. Then attach the circuit coiled white wire to the neutral bar.

MANAGING FUSES

Circuit breakers are much easier to work with, but if your system doesn't overload very often, you may get along just fine with a fuse box.
SHORTED OR OVERLOADED? If a fuse blows, usually it's because too many appliances are running on the same circuit at once—an annoying and potentially dangerous situation. If a fuse blows even though only a normal amount of power is being used by the circuit, the cause could be a short circuit, most often caused by a loose wire; this also is dangerous.

When a fuse blows, take a look at its window. If the cause was overloading, the tab inside will be broken, and the glass will be basically clear. But if the glass is smoky or cloudy and the tab looks burned, chances are it was caused by a short. Check your wiring with the power off. Tighten any loose screws, replace cracked devices, and check for damaged wire ends. If you cannot find the problem, contact an electrician.
HANDLING CARTRIDGE FUSES: Screw-in fuses are generally used for 15- and 20-amp circuits. For larger circuits, cartridge fuses are common. Be very cautious when working near these; some carry as much as 70 amps.

Unless the fuse box is very old, the cartridges will be housed in a fuse block. Shut off the power; the fuse block may itself be the main disconnect. Pull the fuse block out. Use a plastic fuse puller to remove the fuses from the block. Test each cartridge fuse by touching each end with a continuity tester (see page 35). If the tester does not glow, the fuse has blown; replace it.

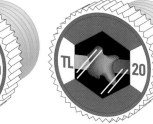

The strip of metal is whole in an unblown fuse (left). If blown, the mica window will be singed (center) or the metal strip will have melted (right), leaving a gap.

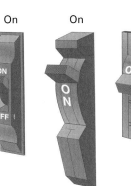

On On Off Off

On Tripped Off

Though breakers may differ slightly in appearance, all clearly show whether a circuit has power or not. Double breakers have a bar connecting the two handles and are used to protect 240-volt circuits.

Not all go to OFF when tripped; some go halfway. To turn the circuit on, switch the breaker all the way OFF, then to ON.

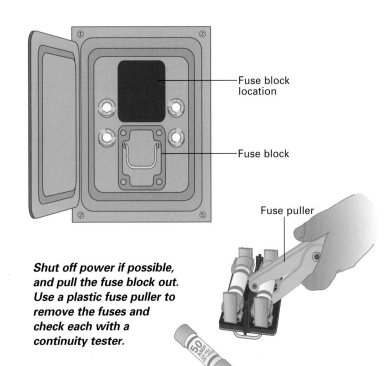

Fuse block location

Fuse block

Fuse puller

Shut off power if possible, and pull the fuse block out. Use a plastic fuse puller to remove the fuses and check each with a continuity tester.

SURGE PROTECTION

Occasionally, the electrical current entering your home may suddenly increase slightly for less than a second. This is called a surge. Static electricity—either from lightning near the power cables outside or from dry carpets inside the home—sometimes is the cause. A surge may also occur when the power company changes from one source of power to another.

Surge-protecting power strip

SURGE DAMAGE:

A surge will not harm lights, fixtures, or other standard household devices; you probably will not even notice it. But some electronic equipment can suffer damage from even a small surge. Computers are the devices most often affected. In most cases, a surge will cause only the loss of some data on your computer. Less often, the computer itself may be seriously harmed.

Other electronic equipment using solid-state circuitry is also vulnerable to power surges. Occasionally, a television may be damaged. Because telephone wires also are subject to static electricity, surge protection for phone lines—especially phone lines that are used by computer modems—is strongly recommended as well.

PROTECTION AGAINST SURGES: A surge protector provides a path—through the ground wire—for the excess electricity to travel so that it will do no harm.

Decide how much of your electrical system needs protection. A device to protect the entire house will not be expensive, but it must be installed between the service head and the panel. This is the time when you should call in a professional. To cover an entire circuit, install a surge arrester in your service panel. It is a small device that clamps to the panel; connect one wire to the breaker and one to the neutral bar.

An even simpler solution is to buy a plug-in power strip, usually holding six to eight outlets. Make sure it protects not only against overloads (like a circuit breaker) but against surges as well. One type doubles as a monitor stand (*below left*) and will help you organize that tangle of cords so often part of the modern home office.

Or, install a surge-protecting receptacle (*below right*). Wire it as you would a standard receptacle with leads connected by wire nuts rather than the house wires attached to terminals.

An under-monitor surge protector helps organize cords while it prevents damage from voltage surges. Some models also protect the telephone line for a modem.

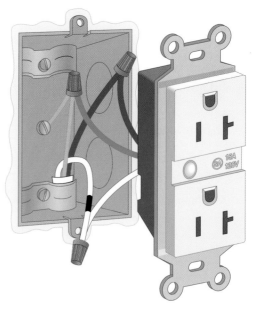

A surge-protecting receptacle is simple to install. The only difficulty you are likely to encounter is overcrowding. A surge-protecting receptacle is about as bulky as a GFCI receptacle.

REPLACING CEILING FIXTURES

You'll need no special skills to install a new ceiling fixture, as long as a ceiling box is in place and anchored firmly enough. Most light fixtures weigh very little, so the box can be supported by the drywall. However, boxes for ceiling fans or heavy chandeliers should be solidly attached to framing (*see page 44*). Choose a replacement fixture with a canopy that will hide any unpainted ceiling area around the box.

Installing recessed canister lights is somewhat more complex (*see pages 86–87*). If you need to wire a new box to a switch, check pages 64–65 and 79–85.

REMOVE THE OLD FIXTURE: Shut off the power to the circuit. (Depending on how the light was wired, turning off the light switch may not shut off all power to the ceiling box.) Remove the globe and the light bulbs. Remove mounting screws and gently pull the canopy down. Inspect the wiring in

the box. Tape wires with minor insulation cracks; replace the wiring if the insulation is generally damaged (*see page 17*).

MOUNT THE HARDWARE: To make sure you will be able to mount the new light, take the stud, nipple, or strap from your box to your hardware store or home center. You'll find hardware to fasten just about any type of fixture to your box.

Most flush-mounted lights simply need a way to fasten the canopy to the ceiling, using a strap or a center stud. Chandeliers are more complicated because the wiring must run through a nipple in the center.

See that the wires are not crammed into the box and do not become twisted during the mounting process. Don't force the canopy in place; rearrange the wires and try again. If the canopy has fiber insulation, resist the temptation to remove it.

Ceiling fixtures attach to boxes with variations on two themes: the strap and the nipple. A strap allows you to attach the canopy with two screws or with a center nipple. For a chandelier, the cord must travel through a center nipple.

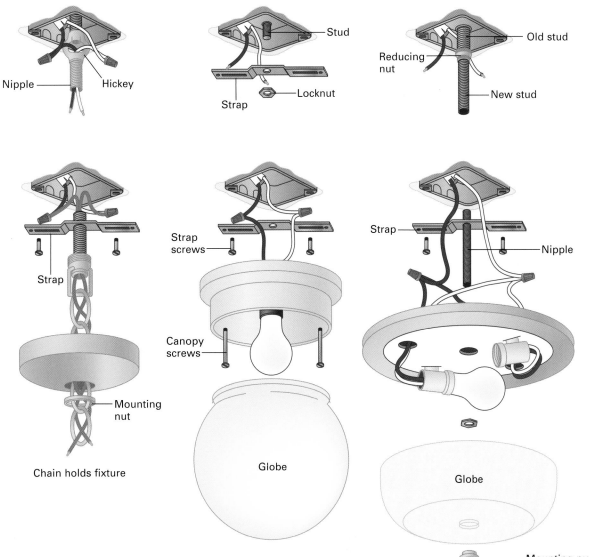

MOUNTING TRACK LIGHTING

Versatile track lighting fixtures provide both general illumination and spot lighting. Some systems allow more than one type of light on the same track; so, for instance, you could combine wide-angle lighting with a spotlight or two.

As a general rule, buy a track that is about two-thirds as long as the ceiling length. Start at a ceiling box, which need not be very strongly anchored. The box can be positioned at one end of the track, or somewhere in the middle.

To install a new ceiling box wired to a switch, see pages 64–65 and 79–85.

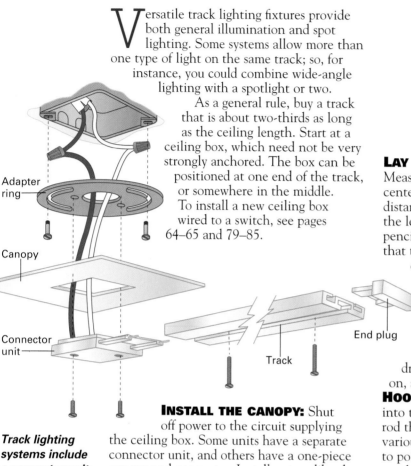

1. *Attach the canopy to the ceiling box using the adapter ring provided with the kit.*

Adapter ring

Canopy

Connector unit

End plug

Track

Track lighting systems include a connector unit and a track. Individual lights usually twist into the track and can be moved or repositioned at will.

INSTALL THE CANOPY: Shut off power to the circuit supplying the ceiling box. Some units have a separate connector unit, and others have a one-piece canopy and connector. Install a strap like that used for standard ceiling fixtures *(see page 41)*, or use an adapter ring like the one shown *(above left)* which allows you to run the track at any angle. Splice the wires (black to black and white to white) with wire nuts, and screw the canopy to the ceiling.

LAY OUT AND ATTACH THE TRACK: Measure from the most visible wall to the center of the canopy. Measure the same distance at two or three other points along the length of the track, and mark with light pencil lines. Stand back and check to see that the line looks parallel to the wall. If you can locate the ceiling joists, and they run perpendicular to the wall, mark their locations.

Connect the track to the connector unit, and have a helper hold the track in position on the ceiling. Drive screws into joists or drywall anchors. Snap the canopy cover on, and restore power to the ceiling box.

HOOK UP LIGHTS: Some track lights twist into the track; others clamp on with a small rod that you push up. Experiment with various light positions. Twist the lights to point in several directions for general overhead lighting, or aim them to highlight certain areas.

2. *Measure from the most visible wall, and mark a light pencil line parallel to it.*

3. *Attach the track to the connector unit, and secure it to the ceiling with screws. Press the end plug in place. Twist individual lights into the track.*

REPAIRING FLUORESCENT LIGHTING

Some newer fluorescent fixtures are very inexpensive, so replacing them is often a better option than repairing them, especially if your ballast has failed. Before replacing, however, make a quick check to see whether the problem is the tube, a lamp socket, the starter (if any), or the ballast.

If a unit suddenly stops working and there is no humming noise, the wall switch or pull chain may be bad (*see pages 31 and 34–35*).

CHECK THE TUBE: Fluorescent tubes last longer than incandescent bulbs, and they usually go bad gradually. If a tube suddenly stops lighting, twist it slightly in both directions; it may work once it seats more securely in the lamp socket.

Look at the tube ends. A new tube will be almost entirely white; an older but still functional tube will have a small amount of gray area. If the end is very dark, it has failed; replace it with one of the same length and wattage.

LAMP SOCKET: The sockets are made of inexpensive plastic and easily become cracked. See that they are firmly anchored to the fixture and that there are no cracks. Compare two sockets to make sure all the little parts are there. If a socket is damaged, turn off the fixture, remove the cover plate, slide the socket out, and disconnect the wires. Replacement sockets are inexpensive.

STARTER: Delayed-start fluorescent fixtures (with lights that flicker a few times before lighting) use small cylindrical starters. If the light flickers for more than a couple of seconds, or if the bulb does not completely light up, remove the bulb and check to see that the starter is screwed in all the way. If the problem persists, replace the starter with one that has the same set of letters and numbers printed on it.

BALLAST: Older units have heavy black ballasts, which step up electrical current to the tube. (Delayed-start fluorescents have a ballast and a starter; rapid-start units have a ballast but no starter.) Newer fixtures have electronic ballasts, which very rarely quit working and are usually impossible to replace.

If the fixture hums, or if you see a dark, gooey substance oozing out, the ballast needs to be replaced. Check the price of a whole new fixture; it may cost less than a replacement ballast.

To remove a ballast, shut off power to the fixture. If the wiring is complex, use pieces of tape for labels. Disconnect wires by unscrewing wire nuts, or by pushing a small screwdriver into the release openings on the lamp sockets. Remove the screws holding the ballast to the fixture. Buy an exact replacement and rewire it.

Starters

Lamp socket

Ballast

Cover plate

A rapid-start fluorescent fixture has a ballast but no starter. Check the lamp and sockets as well as the ballast.

Ballast

Starter

A delayed-start unit is the oldest type. The starter simply twists out and is very easy to replace.

INSTALLING CEILING FANS

A properly installed ceiling fan can cut heating and cooling costs and provide a welcome breeze. In some situations, reversing the fan's direction, so that it pulls air upward, can make a room more uniformly cool or warm.

If you need to install a braced box in a drywall ceiling, cut out a rectangle from joist to joist. Install nailers on each side, and screw the brace ends to the nailers. Install a drywall patch.

INSTALLING A SOLID BOX

Installing a fan is an easy one-day project if you have a ceiling box that is solidly anchored to framing. If you need to install a new box or strengthen an existing box, your time may be more than doubled. Patching the ceiling will require several coats of joint compound, some sanding, and a couple coats of paint.

If you have a plastic ceiling box, the threads will probably not be strong enough to support the fan while it operates. Replace it with a metal box.

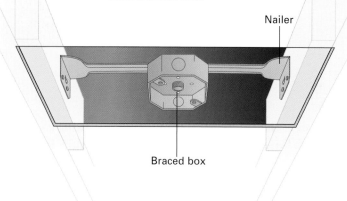

Nailer

Braced box

Wire a new box as you would a standard light box (*see page 79*). The usual arrangement is to have a wall switch supplying power to the fan, while pull chains control whether the light comes on with the fan, as well as the fan's speed. A switch on the fan body determines whether the fan blows air down or pulls it up. You may want to install separate wall switches for the fan and the light. If you want to control the fan's speed from the wall, purchase a special fan switch.

Shut off power to an existing box and test to make sure it is off. Grab the box with a pair of pliers and test for strength. If it wiggles easily, then it will not stand up to a fan's shaking.

WORK FROM ABOVE: If you are fortunate to have an attic (without a floor), work there to save yourself from having to cut and patch the ceiling. If you can't get at the box from above, you may be able to use an expandable brace bar (*see pages 64–65*).

BRACED BOX IN WALLBOARD: To install a new braced box in a wallboard ceiling, cut out a section of ceiling first. See page 64 for instructions.

BRACED BOX IN PLASTER: Plaster lath runs perpendicular to the joists. Cut a channel the width of one lath from joist to joist. Install a braced box, anchoring each end with two drywall screws. Use patching plaster to fill in the channel. Allow it to dry, apply two coats of joint compound, sand smooth, and paint.

1. If the ceiling surface is plaster, cut first with a knife, then use a board and a keyhole saw.

2. Remove one piece of lath, spanning from joist to joist.

3. Patch the channel with patching plaster and then joint compound.

INSTALLING A FAN

This is sometimes painstaking work. Keep careful track of all the little nuts, screws, and washers, and follow the manufacturer's directions. You may need a helper to hold the unit while you complete the wiring.

ATTACH THE BRACKET:
The anchoring bracket must be firm and it must be level, or the fan will wobble. If possible, snug both ends of the bracket up against the ceiling surface, so the bracket is parallel to the ceiling. Drive screws directly into the box, or use a strap (*see page 41*). In some cases, you can anchor the brace with screws driven directly into the framing.

MAKE CONNECTIONS: In most cases, the brace will allow you to hang the motor temporarily, via a hook or a down rod, while you make electrical connections. Hook up wiring for both the fan and the light (if any) by splicing wires and screwing on wire nuts. Don't forget to attach the ground wire.

ATTACH THE MOTOR: Gently push the wires up into the box, where they will stay well out of the way as the motor spins around; use electrical tape to hold them together if necessary. Slip the canopy onto the bracket, and drive the mounting screws to hold it firmly in place.

Test by turning the motor on. Listen carefully to make sure you do not hear the sound of the motor scraping against wires.

Down rod

Motor

Canopy

Light assembly

Globe

Make the electrical connections with the fan hanging temporarily from the bracket. Attach the fan blades, then the light kit, if any.

FAN CLEARANCES

A "ceiling hugging" fan may seem to be a good option, because it does not protrude down into living space and it is less likely to wobble than a fan with a down rod. However, it will simply not do the job. If the fan blades are less than 10 inches away from the ceiling, the fan will not move air effectively. Also see that the blades are kept at least 18 inches from any wall.

Of course, the larger the fan blade, the more air it will circulate. A 42-inch fan will work fine for most bedrooms; for a room larger than 14 feet square, a 52-inch fan will do a better job without having to be turned all the way up.

Also see that the motor does not shake while it turns, even at the highest speed. If it does, use a level to see that the fan is level or that the down rod is plumb, and make sure that it is anchored tightly. If the motor wobbles despite being level and tight, it is defective; return it for a replacement.

ATTACH FAN BLADES AND LIGHT KIT:
Attach each fan blade to its bracket, and attach the brackets to the motor with two screws each. Check that all the screws are tight. If the fan has a separate light kit, make the electrical connections and attach it according to the manufacturer's instructions.

BALANCE A WOBBLY FAN: The fan should remain fairly steady when operating at maximum speed. Don't settle for a wobbly fan; it will only grow worse in time, and it could become dangerous.

First make sure that all the blades are firmly attached to the motor. If they are, then purchase a fan-balancing kit. It will tell you how to test each fan, and it will give you some weights to balance the blades.

REPAIRING DOORBELLS AND CHIMES

Doorbells and chimes use a transformer to lower the current from 120 volts down to the operating voltage of the unit—between 6 and 28 volts. Because the power is so low, bell wire is thin—18- or 20-gauge. There is no need to shut off power while working on a door button, bell, or chime; a "shock" will be barely noticeable. However, remember that standard current flows *into* a transformer; shut off power to the circuit if you will need to open the box to which the transformer is attached.

A doorbell or chime system uses buttons as switches. A transformer steps the power down.

If a bell or chime doesn't sound, first check the button at the door, then the chime or bell mechanism, and finally the transformer.

the wire ends are not broken. Clean the terminals and the wire ends, and reconnect firmly. Push the button to test.

If there is still no sound, strip both ends of a short piece of bell wire. Touch the ends of this "jumper" wire to the terminals (*see below*). If the bell sounds, then the button is defective. Replace it with one that fits in the same place or one that covers the unpainted area where the old button was removed.

If jumping does not produce a sound, jump the terminals again and look carefully for a small spark. If there is a spark, the chime or bell is probably defective. If there is no spark, chances are that the transformer is bad; but check and clean the bell or chime anyway.

CHECK THE BUTTON

If pushing the button produces no sound, remove the small screws holding the button in place; use a knife or a small screwdriver. Wrap the wires loosely with tape so they cannot accidentally slip into the hole while they are disconnected from the button. Examine the wires. Wrap any scraped insulation with electrician's tape. Unscrew the terminals, and check that

Transformer

Front button

Rear button

Plunger

CHECK THE CHIME OR BELL

Remove the chime or bell cover plate. Check for broken wires; sometimes small-gauge wire cracks off near the terminal. Wrap any scraped insulation with electrician's tape. Tighten the terminals and pull gently on the wires to make sure of the connections.

Clean away any dust or debris. Carefully pull back on the plungers to see that they are not jammed; when you release one, it should produce a clear chime. Clean the plunger springs with a toothpick or a cotton swab.

Touch the probes of a voltmeter to the terminals marked "front" and "trans" (transformer). Also touch to "rear" and "trans" if you have a rear button. If power is present within 2 volts of the rating printed on the chime, then the chime is defective; replace it (*see opposite page*).

1. *Remove the button, check the electrical connections, and scrape away any debris.*

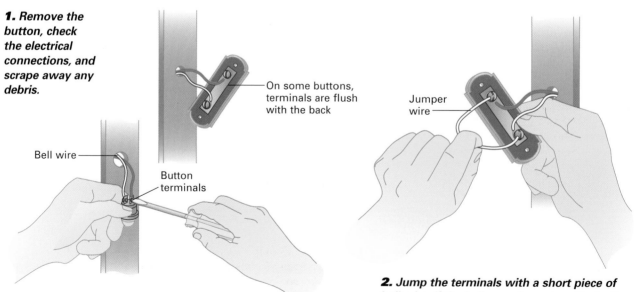

On some buttons, terminals are flush with the back

Bell wire

Button terminals

Jumper wire

2. *Jump the terminals with a short piece of bell wire. If the bell sounds, replace the button.*

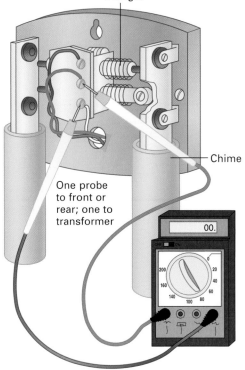

One probe to front or rear; one to transformer

Plunger

Chime

Test a bell or chime with a voltmeter. If the correct amount of power is present but there is no sound, then replace the bell or chime.

REPLACING A CHIME

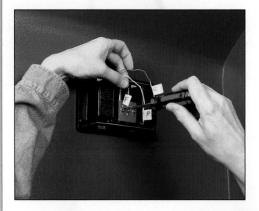

Choose a chime with the same voltage rating as the transformer. Be sure that it will cover any unpainted wall space.

There's no need to shut off power. Use pieces of tape to label the wires for reconnection and to make sure they don't slip back into the wall cavity. Remove screws holding the chime to the wall, and pull it from the wall carefully, slipping the wires out of the housing.

Thread the wires through the new chime and fasten it with screws. Connect the wires and test.

TEST THE TRANSFORMER

Finding the transformer location may be difficult. Bell wires are ordinarily hidden in walls, so you can't follow them. Usually, it will be directly attached to an exposed electrical box. Look next to the service panel, or somewhere (perhaps in the basement) near the button or the chime. There may be other transformers in the house, perhaps for a thermostat or for a low-voltage lighting system. Look for the one with the same voltage rating as your doorbell or chime.
TEST IT: Check the wires and terminals as you did for the button and the bell. Tighten the connections, and test the bell.

Touch the probes of a voltmeter to both terminals. If no power registers, or if the reading is more than 2 volts below the transformer's rating, the transformer is probably faulty.
REPLACING A TRANSFORMER: Before replacing the transformer, make sure power is getting to it. Shut off power to the circuit supplying the transformer. Remove the electrical box's cover plate; you may have to remove the transformer first. Gently pull out the wires, and remove the wire nuts or electrician's tape from the two splices that connect to the transformer. Restore power,

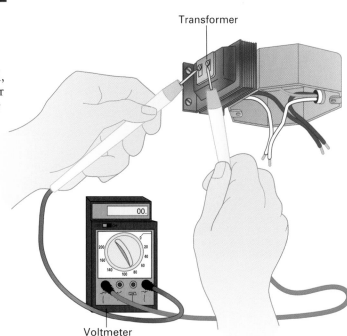

Transformer

Voltmeter

Test a transformer with a voltmeter. Readings should be within 2 volts of the transformer's rating. Also see that power is going to the transformer by testing for power in the box.

REPAIRING DOORBELLS AND CHIMES
continued

and test touch the probes of a neon tester or a voltmeter. If no power is present, the house wiring may be faulty.

WATCH THE RATINGS: Purchase a transformer with the same voltage rating as the old one. Shut off power to the circuit. Attach the new transformer to the box; connect the wires in the box, as well as the low-voltage wires. Restore power and test the doorbell.

CHECK THE WIRING

Occasionally a bell wire breaks. This can be very difficult to diagnose, because the bell wires are usually hidden inside walls.

FIND THE BREAK: First, look in places where a break is most likely to occur: Where the wiring enters wood molding or exits out of a wall, for instance. If you have done remodeling work recently, perhaps you poked through a wire with a nail or damaged a wire when you removed a board. A battery-powered multi-tester will tell you if a wire has a break.

RUNNING NEW WIRES: Running new wires in the same location as the old ones may not be worth the trouble. (Remember, the wiring was probably run before the wallboard or plaster was installed.) However, if the wiring run is short, you may only need to drill a single hole.

You also may have to remove pieces of molding. If the old wire is damaged rather than broken, you may be able to use it as a fish tape: Splice and tape the new wire to the old, and pull the old through. Often, however, old wire binds up and won't work as a fish tape. Even if the new wire is exposed, it is thin enough that it may not be noticeable.

Spark indicates transformer is working

If the transformer is working but power is not reaching the button or the chime, then a wire may be broken. To test whether you have fixed the problem, touch the ends of wires and look for a spark.

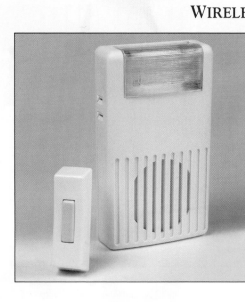

WIRELESS CHIMES

If your bell wiring is defective, you face the surprisingly difficult job of pulling new bell wire. (Because bell wire is so thin, it tends to bind and break if you attempt to use old wire to pull in new wire.) To avoid this, or if you want to install a chime in a new location, consider installing a wireless unit. These affordable systems will not only save you the chore of running wires, they will eliminate the need for a transformer as well.

The chime must be plugged into a receptacle. The button is battery-operated, and slightly larger than a standard wired button. Simply mount the chime, plug it in, and attach the button to the house.

MAINTAINING THERMOSTATS

A thermostat is a heat-sensitive switch that turns a heating or air conditioning unit on and off when the air temperature becomes warmer or cooler than the programmed levels.

INSPECT AND CLEAN: Dust will collect in a thermostat and cause it to misfire. Pull the cover off and clean the thermostat by blowing on it and brushing off dust and dead insects with a fine-bristled brush (don't use a toothbrush).

TROUBLESHOOT THE WIRING: There is no need to turn off the power; the voltage is very low. Remove the screw(s) holding the thermostat body to the wall plate, and pull the body away. Clean the terminals and see that all the wires are firmly connected. Check that the wall plate is firmly anchored and level; tilting can disrupt the settings.

If the thermostat does not switch on, use a short piece of wire with stripped ends to jump the terminals. In many systems, connecting "R" to "W" will turn the burner on, and connecting "Y" to "G" will turn on the blower. If they do turn on, the thermostat is defective; replace it.

If no power is present, find the transformer and test it as you would a doorbell transformer (*see pages 47–48*).

PROGRAMMABLE THERMOSTAT

Various programmable thermostats are available. Some control both heating and cooling and can be set to turn on at the same time each day or at different times in the same day. Check with your heating company to see whether such a unit will really save you money. For instance, a system that heats slowly will have to work hard to recover from lower nighttime temperatures. When you go on vacation, program the system to use minimal energy while you're gone and to heat up the house for your homecoming. Before buying one, see whether you will have to run extra wires.

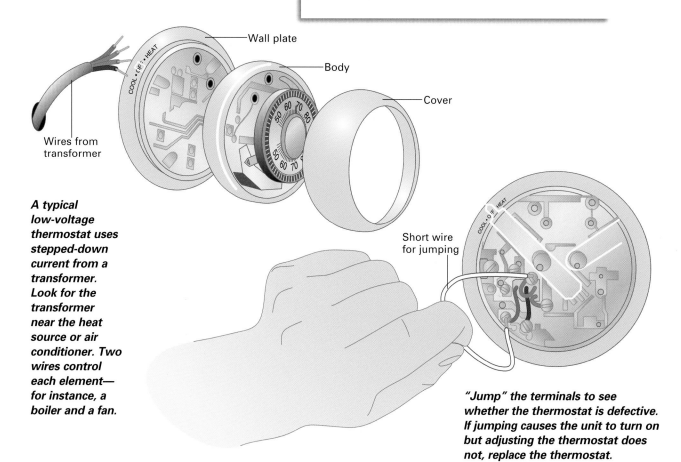

Wall plate

Body

Cover

Wires from transformer

A typical low-voltage thermostat uses stepped-down current from a transformer. Look for the transformer near the heat source or air conditioner. Two wires control each element— for instance, a boiler and a fan.

Short wire for jumping

"Jump" the terminals to see whether the thermostat is defective. If jumping causes the unit to turn on but adjusting the thermostat does not, replace the thermostat.

UNDER-CABINET HALOGEN LIGHTS

If you plan to install new kitchen cabinets, you can run standard cables through the walls and install under-cabinet fluorescent fixtures controlled by a standard switch. But low-voltage halogen lights are much easier to install, especially if the cabinets are already in place.

PLAN THE SYSTEM: Under-cabinet lights should illuminate the countertop below them without causing glare. As a general rule, one 20-watt halogen light every 2 to 3 feet will provide ample illumination. Place at least one light directly above the sink and anywhere else you often work—for example, beside the range, or above a built-in cutting board.

Most lights have slightly recessed bulbs that reduce glare. If the bottom of the wall cabinet is a standard 54 inches above the floor, lights placed near the wall will not shine in the eyes of an average-sized adult. Experiment to be sure. If glare is a problem, install a baffle—a strip of 1×2 running under the front of the cabinets—to act as a shade.

Another reason to place the lights near the rear wall is to keep heat away from anyone working in your kitchen. The lights become very hot. Don't place a light near flammables or in locations accessible to children.

WIRE THE TRANSFORMER: Inside a cabinet, near a receptacle and in a spot where the components won't get bumped, screw the power block and transformer to the cabinet wall. Drill a hole in the bottom of the cabinet so you can run the power cord to the receptacle. Wire the power block to the transformer.

MOUNT THE LIGHTS: Drill smaller holes in the bottom of the cabinet for the wires that run to the lights. Plan to run wires inside the cabinets, or along the undersides. Because the wires are thin and flexible, they can be easily hidden.

Attach the lamp bases to the underside of the cabinets. Choose the screw sizes carefully: They should anchor the bases firmly without poking through the cabinet. Run wires from the power block to the lamp bases. Use small rounded staples to snug them into corners—they will be unobtrusive and out of harm's way. The wires cannot be cut, so you will end up with coils of wire that need to be hidden inside the cabinet.

At each light, plug in a bulb and snap on the lens cover.

INSTALL THE SWITCH: Place a battery in the switch body, and mount it in a convenient location on the wall. Use screws with plastic or drywall anchors if you cannot attach to a stud. Attach the cover plate, plug in the transformer, and test the system.

Attractive halogen fixtures can be suspended from soffits or ceilings. All require a transformer.

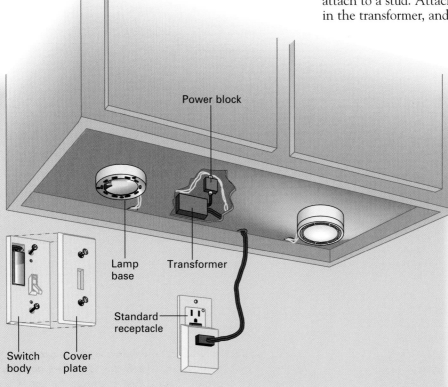

Power block
Lamp base
Transformer
Standard receptacle
Switch body
Cover plate

An under-cabinet halogen system consists of lights, a transformer and power block, and a battery-operated switch. Installation is easy: Mount the switch wherever you choose, run thin wires to each light, and plug in the transformer.

LOW-VOLTAGE OUTDOOR LIGHTING

Here's a way to provide pleasant illumination to outdoor areas for a small amount of money and a minimum of hassle. There are no trenches to dig and no 125-watt cable to run. Low-voltage wiring means no worries during and after installation.

You can purchase most of the components in a kit. Some kits come with a timer or a photovoltaic sensor to turn lights on at night and off during the day.

TRANSFORMER LOCATION: If you have an exterior receptacle, mount the transformer near it. Attach the transformer to the house, at least 3 feet above ground level. (If you have no exterior receptacle, see page 92 for instructions on installing one. Or, drill a hole through the exterior wall, install the transformer inside the house, and run the low-voltage cable out through the hole.)

INSTALL THE LIGHTS: Scatter the lights where you want them on the yard. Run the cable to them, burying it as you go. (Pry up sod and slip the cable in, dig a shallow trench, or cover the cable with mulch when you're finished.)

Attach the wire to the snap-on connectors at each light. Poke each light into the soil. If the ground is hard, you may have to dig a starter hole. Plug the transformer in.

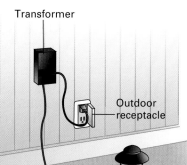

BRICK LIGHTING

For understated outdoor lighting along walkways, consider illuminated plastic bricks. Some come as part of paver-like plastic edging systems (*shown above*), others install along with brick pavers. Like other types of outdoor lighting, these bricks are powered by a timer/transformer.

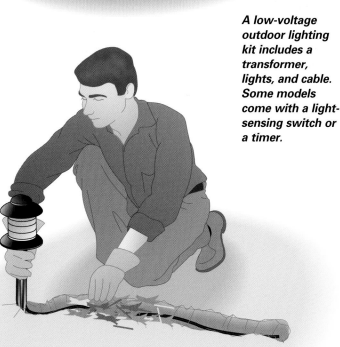

A low-voltage outdoor lighting kit includes a transformer, lights, and cable. Some models come with a light-sensing switch or a timer.

The thin low-voltage cable does not need to be protected against weather and it does not pose a threat from shocks. Just keep it out of sight and out of harm's way.

RUNNING NEW LINES

Whenever you plan for new circuits, even if you're only adding a single light fixture or receptacle, be sure that you will not overload the circuit. An overloaded circuit will not only annoy you with blown fuses or tripped breakers, but it can be dangerous as well. The information on pages 70–71 will help you decide whether you need to run cable all the way to the service panel, or whether you can simply add onto an existing line.

Working with nonmetallic cable is very easy—the only skill you have to learn is how to strip wires safely. Working with BX and Greenfield (flexible conduit) is nearly as simple—you only have to learn to cut through their armored sheathings without damaging wires. Pages 54–59 show how to make these installations quickly and safely.

Installing new lines while remodeling will require carpentry and wall preparation skills. You may spend far more time patching holes than you spend doing the electrical work. For extensive work, such as a kitchen remodel, you can often save time and end up with a cleaner-looking job if you remove all the drywall or plaster from a wall or even the whole room, rather than cutting out sections. With the walls free and clear, electrical work is easier— and hanging new drywall may be faster than patching. However, it is often possible to install one or two new fixtures without doing much cutting; pages 60–66 show you how.

KITCHEN ELECTRICAL LINES

In most homes, the kitchen uses the most electricity of any room. Aside from air conditioners and an electric clothes dryer, the refrigerator usually is the single largest user of power. Avoid repeated overloads by providing plenty of circuitry. Many local codes call for at least one 15-amp lighting circuit dedicated only to the kitchen, two 20-amp circuits for receptacles, and separate circuits for the dishwasher and garbage disposer. An electric range requires its own 250-amp circuit.

A typical kitchen is a maze of electrical appliances, fixtures, and receptacles—if you are planning a kitchen upgrade, you'll very likely need to run new electrical lines. Lighting may include overhead and under-cabinet fixtures, as well as lights for eating and working areas. The dishwasher, garbage disposer, hot-water dispenser, and range hood all are hard-wired. The refrigerator, microwave, and various cooking appliances all need 20-amp receptacles.

IN THIS CHAPTER

Working with Armored Cable (BX) **54**

Running Wires in Conduit or Greenfield **56**

Running Cable in Unfinished Spaces **58**

Running Cable in Attics and Basements **60**

Installing Boxes in Finished Walls **62**

Installing Ceiling Boxes **64**

Running Cable in Finished Spaces **66**

Raceway Wiring **69**

Planning New Circuits **70**

Adding New Circuits **72**

Telephone and Cable Wiring **74**

WORKING WITH ARMORED CABLE (BX)

Years ago, BX was the most common type of electrical cable for residential buildings because it protects fairly well against nails, yet is flexible. In fact, when it first became available for houses, installers preferred BX because it could be retrofitted behind moldings and through finished walls in existing buildings.

Today, nonmetallic (NM) cable has largely replaced BX as the cable of choice. But some local codes still call for armored cable, especially when it is semiexposed (*see below*). Use BX wherever a line might be bumped, scraped, or pinched; for short runs outside of walls, under sinks, and in utility areas like workshops or hobby areas; or, if code permits, inside a garage or farm building. Though BX provides much more protection than NM cable, you should run it where nails and fasteners won't pierce it. A nail or screw driven directly into it will damage the wires.

BX cutter

HOW TO CUT BX

Cut the armor on the BX shorter than the wires inside. Often this means making two cuts—one for overall length and one to expose 8 inches or so of wires. Whichever method you use, take care that you do not nick wire insulation while cutting the armor, and that the cut end of the armor does not have sharp edges that will nick insulation.

BX CUTTER: Buy one of these if you will be doing a lot of work with BX. Adjust the cutter for the size of cable, and slip the cable in. Rotate the arm to make a lengthwise cut through the armor.

BEND AND SNIP: If you have the hand strength, bend the armor over until it snaps; it will not break, but it will come slightly unraveled at one point. Twist the waste side clockwise (against the windings of the armor) to unravel the armor further. Use a pair of tin snips to cut through the armor, and pull the waste end off. Then trim the cut end so that no sharp edges can damage wiring insulation.

Use BX when the cable is semiexposed: inside a cabinet, under a sink, or in a closet.

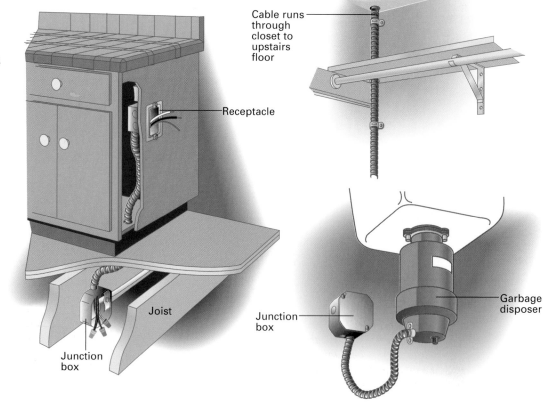

Cable runs through closet to upstairs floor

Receptacle

Joist

Junction box

Junction box

Garbage disposer

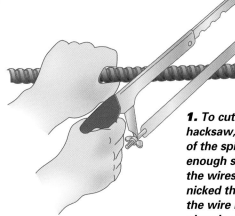

1. To cut BX with a hacksaw, saw into one of the spiral ridges enough so you can see the wires but haven't nicked them. If you cut the wire insulation the piece is unuseable.

2. Twist back and forth until the ridge breaks and the armor comes free.

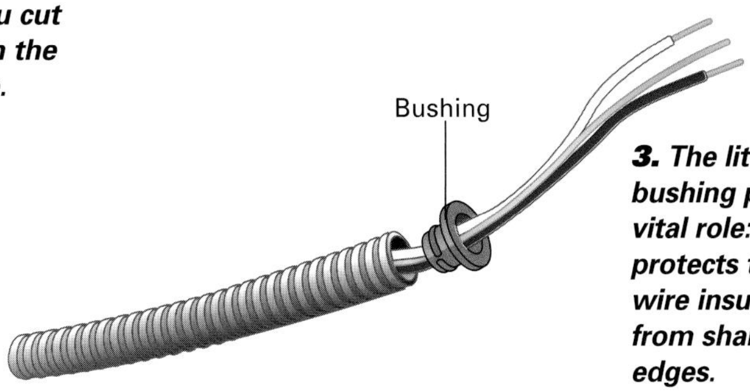

Bushing

3. The little red bushing plays a vital role: It protects the wire insulation from sharp edges.

CUT WITH A HACKSAW: Hold the hacksaw blades at right angles to the armor's spirals, and cut carefully, just barely through the armor so you do not damage the insulation. You don't have to cut all the way around, only through one portion of the winding. With your hands or two pairs of pliers, twist the armor back and forth until it snaps free, and pull the waste piece off.

SECURING THE CABLE

Thread BX through holes in the centers of studs, or protect it with metal plates, as you would for NM cable (*see pages 58–59*). Wherever the cable is exposed, clamp it with straps every few feet.

BUSHINGS PREVENT CUTS: Pull off the paper that wraps the wires. If the cable contains an aluminum bonding strip, snip it so it is about an inch long, and fold it back against the armor. Slip a special plastic bushing, usually red, over the wires, and slide it into the armor. This bushing is very important because it protects wire insulation from the sharp ends of the armor.

CLAMP IT: Slide a connector onto the end of the cable, and tighten the setscrew or clamp. Make the connection firm and secure, especially if the armor will act as the ground. Thread the wires through a knockout hole in the electrical box. Slide the locknut over the wires, and screw it onto the connector.

Tighten the locknut by tapping it with a hammer and a screwdriver. Quickly check to see that all connections are tight.

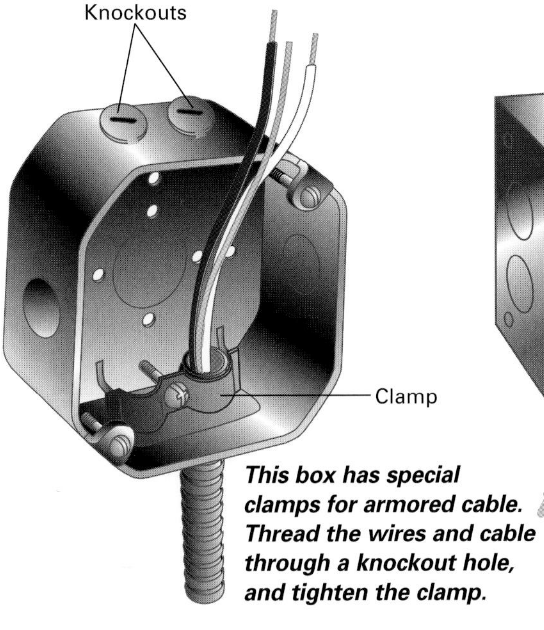

Knockouts

Clamp

This box has special clamps for armored cable. Thread the wires and cable through a knockout hole, and tighten the clamp.

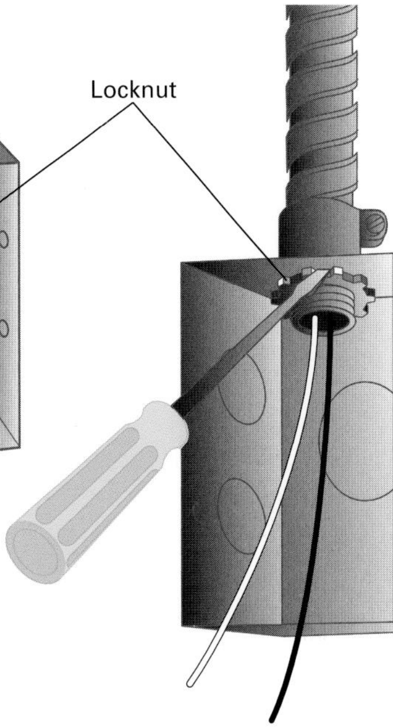

Locknut

Install a BX connector on the armor, slip the wires through a knockout hole, and secure the connector with a locknut. Tighten the locknut with a screwdriver.

RUNNING WIRES IN CONDUIT OR GREENFIELD

Installing conduit and Greenfield (flexible conduit—essentially BX without wires) is more expensive and time-consuming than running NM cable or BX. However, conduit has two distinct advantages. First, it provides solid protection for the wires, and local codes sometimes require it when wiring is exposed. Second, conduit makes it easy to rewire later, should you decide to change service; new wires can be pulled through old conduit. Most commercial electrical work is done with conduit. Don't be intimidated by it. With a bit of practice and a conduit bender, you can install runs just as tight and neat looking as those made by the pros.

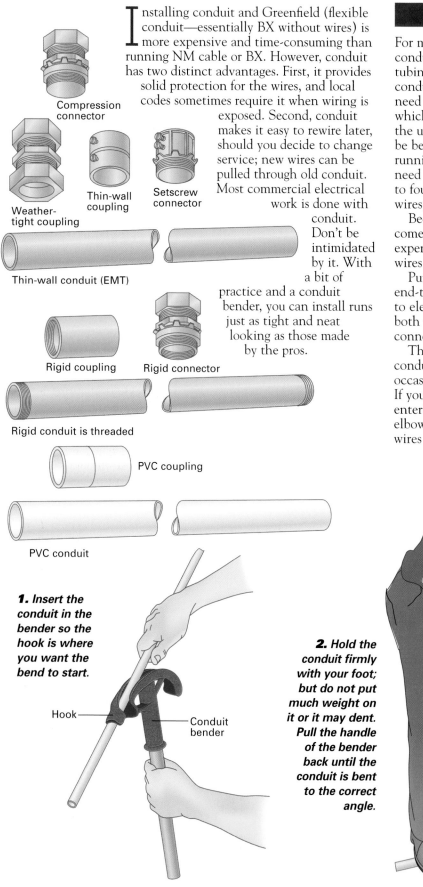

Compression connector

Weather-tight coupling

Thin-wall coupling

Setscrew connector

Thin-wall conduit (EMT)

Rigid coupling

Rigid connector

Rigid conduit is threaded

PVC coupling

PVC conduit

1. *Insert the conduit in the bender so the hook is where you want the bend to start.*

Hook

Conduit bender

2. *Hold the conduit firmly with your foot; but do not put much weight on it or it may dent. Pull the handle of the bender back until the conduit is bent to the correct angle.*

CHOOSING THE PARTS

For most residential work, use thin-wall conduit, also called EMT (electrical metal tubing). Some codes call for intermediate conduit (IMC) and for outside work you may need to use galvanized rigid conduit (GRC), which cannot be bent. Some codes also allow the use of plastic PVC conduit, which cannot be bent. PVC conduit is especially useful for running cable underground. Typically, you'll need to use ½-inch conduit when running up to four wires, and ¾-inch conduit for more wires; local codes have specific requirements.

Because Greenfield requires no bending, it comes in handy in tight locations. It is expensive, however, and cannot hold as many wires as conduit can.

Purchase couplings to join conduit sections end-to-end, and connectors to attach conduit to electrical boxes. If the conduit and the box both will be attached to the wall, use an offset connector (*see opposite page*).

The best way to make a turn is to bend the conduit with a conduit bender, but occasionally you may need to use an elbow. If you will make more than three turns before entering a junction box, install a pulling elbow (*see opposite page*) so you can pull the wires into it and start again.

RUNNING CONDUIT

Fasten one electrical box in place as a starting point. Add connectors and cut conduit to reach the next box. Fasten the box in place before attaching the conduit. Continuing in the same fashion, complete the installation for the entire run.

MEASURE AND BEND: Purchase a bender made for your conduit size. Because the bend will not be sharp, take into account the bend distance— 5 inches for ½-inch conduit and 6 inches for ¾-inch—when measuring.

Offset connector

ADD A PULLING ELBOW

Strategically placed pulling elbows make fishing wires through conduit easier. Install one after every three bends, if possible. Never make electrical connections inside a pulling elbow; wires must pass through unbroken.

Don't try to measure precisely; cut the conduit a bit long on each end, hold it in position, and mark for exact cuts.

Slip the conduit through the bender, with the bender's hook at the beginning of the bend. Place the conduit on the floor, brace it with your foot, and pull steadily. Tugging may produce a crimp, which will make it difficult to pull the wires through.

CUT: Burrs on the inside of a cut can scrape wire insulation, so use a tubing cutter rather than a hacksaw. Clamp it fairly tight, rotate, tighten more, and repeat until the cut is complete. Use the tubing cutter's reamer and a file to remove rough edges.

CONNECT: Use compression or setscrew fittings to join pieces together and to enter boxes. Clamp the conduit firmly with straps every few feet.

PULLING WIRES

This can be hard physical labor, especially if the wires are tightly packed. Lubricate the wires with pulling grease to ease the job.

Beginning at a box or a pulling elbow, thread the tape backwards to the entry point. Attach the wires to the tape by bending them over. Wrap tightly with tape so that the splice can slide easily through the conduit.

Have a helper feed the tape and then the wires through the entry point while you pull at the exit point. Make sure to leave 8 to 10 inches of wire in each box so that you'll have plenty of wire for splicing and connecting.

Feed the wires

Pull the tape

Install all of the conduit, then pull the wires through. If you have more than three bends (as shown), install a pulling elbow to make the pulling easier. Push the tape through the conduit, and join the wire ends to the tape by folding them over and wrapping with tape. Then one person feeds the wires through while the other pulls the tape.

RUNNING CABLE IN UNFINISHED SPACES

I f you are fortunate enough to have framed walls with no drywall or plaster installed, wiring will be much easier than it would be in a finished space.

Wiring is frail and vulnerable. If you're remodeling, install it after you have finished the framing, roughed in your plumbing lines, and installed all ductwork.

ANCHORING BOXES

Install all the wall and ceiling boxes first, then run cable between them. (*See page 21 for box options.*)

SELECT BOXES: Choose boxes that are easy to install so that they will be flush with the finished wall surface—usually ½ inch out from the framing. "Nail-on" boxes install in a flash. Most residential electrical work is done with inexpensive plastic boxes. If a box has to be extra strong—for instance, if it will support a chandelier or ceiling fan—use a metal box anchored to two framing members.

Purchase single switch/receptacle boxes, ceiling boxes, and junction boxes. Buy "two-gang" or "three-gang" boxes where you will install more than one switch or receptacle.

INSTALL: Position all switch and receptacle boxes at uniform heights. The most common arrangement is to have switches 48 inches and receptacles 12–16 inches from

Run cable through holes in the centers of the studs, or cover notched cables with protective metal plates.

the floor. Your local building code probably dictates where you place receptacles. If not, place them at least every 12 feet so that the cord of a lamp or appliance placed near a wall need extend only six feet to be plugged in.

Place a single ceiling box in the center of the room, or if you're installing more than one ceiling fixture, space their boxes evenly. Recessed canister lights have built-in boxes.

DRILLING HOLES

Notches on lumber weaken framing and make the cable vulnerable to puncture. Instead, drill holes whenever possible.

HOLE PLACEMENT: Bore holes in the centers of studs, so the edges are not less than 1¼ inches from the edge of the framing. If the hole is closer to the edge, or if you have to make a notch instead of a hole (where wiring

Protective metal plate

Insulated cable staple

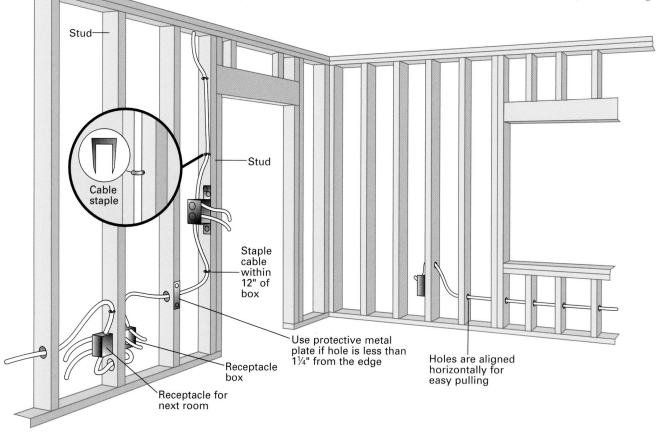

Stud

Stud

Cable staple

Staple cable within 12" of box

Use protective metal plate if hole is less than 1¼" from the edge

Holes are aligned horizontally for easy pulling

Receptacle box

Receptacle for next room

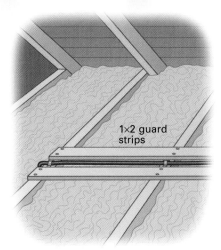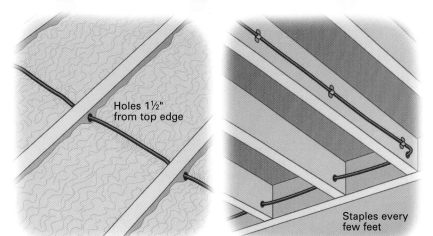

In an attic, protect cable with guard strips that are at least as thick as the cable.

If you plan to finish an attic floor, run cable through holes that are at least 1½ inches from the top edge.

Run basement cable through holes—don't attach it to the underside of joists.

must go through corner framing, for example), protect the cable from nails by installing a protective metal plate.

Keep the holes aligned to make it easier to pull cable through later. Snap a chalk line to provide a guide.

DRILLING TIPS: Use a ¾-inch drill bit for standard NM or BX cable. A Forstner bit costs more but makes for easier drilling than a spade bit. If you have a lot of holes to drill, rent a professional-grade right-angle drill, which can run all day without burning out and will make it easy to drill straight holes.

PULLING AND ATTACHING CABLE

Pull long cable runs first, and use leftover short lengths for runs between boxes. Don't permit the cable to sag more than an inch between holes. Don't bend cable sharply.

STAPLE TO FRAMING: Use cable staples to hold NM or BX against the sides of framing members. Read the packaging to make sure the staples are designed for your type of cable. Insulated staples cost a bit more but won't bite into the sheathing. Secure cable every 4 feet or so where it does not run through holes, and within 12 inches of every box or panel where clamps are used to secure the cable. If you use a box that has no clamp, secure the cable within 8 inches of the box.

PREPARING THE CABLE: Leave 8 inches or so of free cable inside each box. For NM cable, use a cable ripper (*see page 25*) to remove enough sheathing so ½ inch of sheathing remains inside the box. Number cables to indicate which circuit they are on.

Cut BX cable with a BX cutter. Some codes require that you leave a 6- to 8-inch loop of cable next to each box. That way, if you make a mistake in stripping the cable or wires, you can pull more cable through and start again.

CABLE-CAPTURING OPTIONS

The ceiling fixture box (*left*) has flexible tabs that make it possible to push the cable through but keep it from pulling out. Strip the sheathing and insulation, and poke the cable through. An attach bar can be readily nailed to joists. The box (*right*) has no clamp. Anchor the cable with an insulated staple within 8 inches of an unclamped box.

Running Cable in Attics and Basements

Fish tape

Electronic stud sensor

Running cable in a room with finished walls is altogether different and much more difficult than installing it in a room with exposed framing (*see pages 58–59*). Plan carefully to minimize damage to the walls. If you have an unfinished basement below or an attic above, work from these areas whenever possible.

For instructions on connecting a new receptacle to existing wiring, see page 78.

Two Useful Tools

Two special tools are necessary for running cable inside finished walls: an electronic stud finder and a fish tape.

An electronic stud finder is more reliable than a magnetic stud finder. With it, you can map wall interiors without having to drill exploratory holes. Use it to find not only studs but also horizontal blocking and other framing obstacles inside the wall.

Purchase a fish tape made of flat metal, 1/8 inch wide and 1/16 inch thick. One fish tape on the job is good; two is much better. One tape lets you fish from a small or large opening into a larger area—for example, from a small hole in the top plates down to a box cutout in the wall or between floor joists.

Two tapes can be hooked together in cavities where the arch in one tape would make it difficult to hit the location below.

Cabling from the Attic

If the attic above is unfinished, lay down pieces of plywood so you won't have to worry about accidentally stepping between joists and putting a hole in the ceiling.

Cut the hole for the switch or receptacle box. Make a locator hole in

1. Push a piece of wire through a hole directly above the box cutout to mark the spot in the attic.

Wire or bent coat hanger

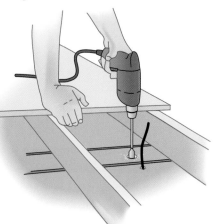

2. Drill a ¾" hole through the top plate of the wall near the locator hole.

3. Feed one fish tape down through the attic and another fish tape up through the box cutout. Hook the tapes together, and pull the lower tape up into the attic.

Fish tapes hook inside wall

4. Hook the cable to the fish tape, and pull it down through the box hole.

Cable

the ceiling directly above where you want the new outlet or switch. Push a piece of wire through the locator hole.

Go into the attic, find the wire, and drill a ³⁄₄-inch hole through the top plate of the wall near the locator hole. Nail heads in the top plate usually show you the location of studs so don't drill there. Plan to run the cable down between the studs to the new box location.

Thread fish tape down through the hole in the attic while a helper threads another tape up through the box cutout. Have the person in the attic rotate the tape while the person below moves the lower tape up and down. The tapes will hook together. Pull the lower tape up into the attic. Attach the cable to the fish tape, and have the helper pull it down through the box cutout.

Some older houses have fire blocking—short horizontal 2×4s that run between studs. Use a stud finder to find the blocking. Cut a notch in the wall and the blocking so you can run cable through. Protect the cable with a metal plate, and patch the wall.

CABLING FROM THE BASEMENT

If you will be installing a wall receptacle by bringing cable from below, drill a locator hole directly under the new outlet and insert a piece of wire down through it. The bottom plate will not be visible like a top plate in an attic; measure carefully to find the center of the wall's bottom plate.

Drill a ³⁄₄-inch hole up through the subfloor and the plate. Run cable through holes in the center of the joists to the ³⁄₄-inch hole. Strip the cable sheathing, twist the wires together, and bend the ends into a loop. Have a helper push the cable up through the hole while you run a fish tape through the receptacle hole. When they hook together, pull the cable up.

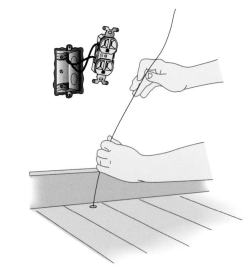

1. Drill a small locator hole directly below an existing receptacle and push a piece of wire through it.

2. Measure from the wire to the center of the bottom plate and drill a ³⁄₄" hole through the subfloor and the plate.

3. Form the cable end into a hook and connect it to a fish tape from above.

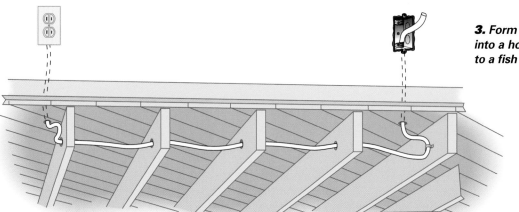

4. If the cable runs perpendicular to the joists, run it through ³⁄₄" holes in the center of the joists.

INSTALLING BOXES IN FINISHED WALLS

Cutting holes and installing boxes in finished walls is relatively simple; pulling the cable to the box is more difficult. Here's how to install the boxes in the walls you'll typically encounter. Once you've cut a hole and before installing the box, you'll need to run the cable (*see pages 60–61 and 66–68*).

MARK THE LOCATION: Position all the boxes in a room at consistent heights: 48 inches from the floor for switches and 12 to 16 inches up for receptacle boxes.

Old-work boxes are designed to attach to wallboard or plaster—not to a stud. They will hold firmly enough for most purposes. If a box needs to be extra strong, cut the hole next to a stud, and drive screws through the box into the stud. (Some boxes have hardware that makes it impossible to snug up against a stud.) Avoid positioning a box directly on the face of a stud; notching the stud will be difficult.

Use a stud sensor or drill a small hole and explore the potential box location with a bent piece of wire to check for obstructions. Use a carpenter's level to position the box plumb and level against the wall. If your box does not come with a cardboard template, trace around it so you'll know where to cut.

CUT THE HOLE: Old-work boxes need precise holes to fasten tightly. Take note of how the box attaches to the wall, and do not cut the hole too wide. The box flanges must grab the wall surface.

For wallboard, cut the outline with a utility knife, using a straightedge as a guide. Then cut to the inside of the knife incision with a keyhole saw or saber saw for a precise, cleanly cut hole. When you run cable, take care not to damage the hole: Even a slight gouge can keep a box from fitting snugly.

For plaster, avoid cracking the surrounding wall area. Some lath-and-plaster walls are firmer than others. Often it helps to tape the surrounding area. Score the outline several times with a knife, and then cut with a keyhole saw. To be extra safe, cut all the way through the plaster with the knife. If the lath flexes while sawing, you may crack the wall. For that reason, many electricians prefer a keyhole saw to a power saw, because it's easier to stop cutting if you see the wall is bouncing. If you use a saber saw, press it firmly against the wall to minimize vibration.

FASTEN THE BOX: Several common boxes are shown (*right*). Plastic boxes are easier to install; but in an old house that uses armored cable for a ground, you must install a metal box. Purchase two or more types to find out which works best in your situation.

PLASTIC BOX IN WALLBOARD

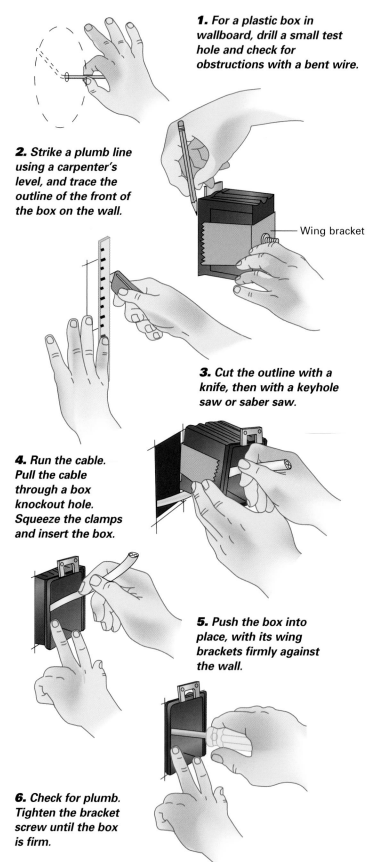

1. For a plastic box in wallboard, drill a small test hole and check for obstructions with a bent wire.

2. Strike a plumb line using a carpenter's level, and trace the outline of the front of the box on the wall.

Wing bracket

3. Cut the outline with a knife, then with a keyhole saw or saber saw.

4. Run the cable. Pull the cable through a box knockout hole. Squeeze the clamps and insert the box.

5. Push the box into place, with its wing brackets firmly against the wall.

6. Check for plumb. Tighten the bracket screw until the box is firm.

METAL BOX IN PLASTER AND LATH

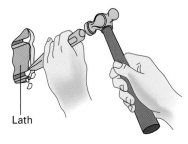

Lath

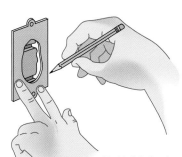

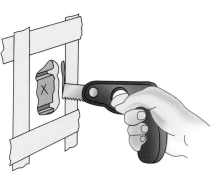

1. To install a metal box in a plaster wall, chisel plaster from the full width of one lath.

2. Hold the box or a cardboard template plumb against the wall, and trace around it.

3. Place masking tape around the outline, score the outline with a knife, and cut to the inside of the incision with a keyhole saw or saber saw. Run cable to the hole.

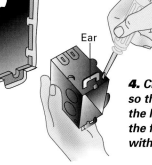

Ear

4. Chip away a little plaster so the box ears fit against the lath. Adjust the ears so the face of the box is flush with the wall surface.

5. Pull cable through the knockout, and clamp it. Drill pilot holes and screw the box to the lath.

METAL BOX IN PANELING

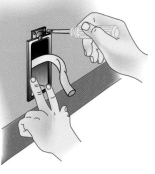

1. To install a box in a wall with paneling ⅜" thick or thicker, trace the outline of the box.

2. Drill holes in the corners and just outside the outline at the top and bottom center. Cut with a saber saw or keyhole saw.

3. Attach the box directly to the wood by drilling pilot holes and driving small screws through the ears.

METAL BOX IN THIN PANELING

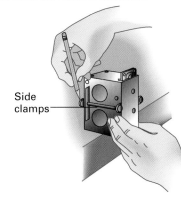

Side clamps

1. If the paneling is thinner than ⅜", use a box with side clamps. Mark and cut notches on the side.

2. Pull the cable through. Hold the box tight against the wall and tighten the clamp screws.

INSTALLING NEW CEILING BOXES

Wing

Flange

Old-work ceiling box

To install new boxes in ceilings, first cut holes, run cable (*see pages 60–61 and 66–68*), and then install the boxes. Note that while not all codes require that lights be grounded, a ceiling fan must be grounded.

If you're installing a single light, center its box on the ceiling. Test to see whether there is a joist in the way by using an electronic stud sensor (*see page 60*) or by drilling a small hole and inserting a piece of bent wire. If you have to move the box a couple of inches off center to get away from the face of the joist, it will probably not be noticeable.

If you want more than one overhead light in a room, recessed canister lights are unobtrusive (*see pages 86–87*).

OLD-WORK BOXES

If your ceiling box will hold a light fixture that weighs only a few pounds, use an old-work box that holds the box with clamps behind the ceiling surface. Several options are available; all use clamping systems similar to those used for wall boxes. The old-work box *above left* is an ideal choice.

Cut the hole precisely—use the cardboard template that comes with the box. Run the cable, and pull it through the box. Push the box up into the hole, its flange flush with the ceiling surface. As you tighten each of the two screws, a wing rotates out, then moves down to clasp the box to the wallboard or plaster.

BRACED BOXES

To install a heavy chandelier or a ceiling fan, you'll need a braced box. You have several options.

BOX WITH BRACKET: Cut a hole about 8 inches square between the joists where the box will be located. Using a tape measure, measure the distance to the joists on each side of the hole. Use a framing square and knife to cut the wallboard paper in a rectangle that spans from joist to joist. Cut the rectangle with a saber saw or

1. For a braced box in a wallboard ceiling, cut an 8"-square hole and then measure for a rectangle spanning the joists. Cut the opening and trim the edges.

2. Install cleats on both joists with the bottom edges on top of the wallboard. Trim away any loose edges.

3. Cut a wallboard patch, ¼" smaller than the opening, and cut out an opening for the box.

4. Run cable into the box and fasten the brace. Attach the patch with wallboard screws. Apply mesh tape and several coats of joint compound to the patch. Sand and paint.

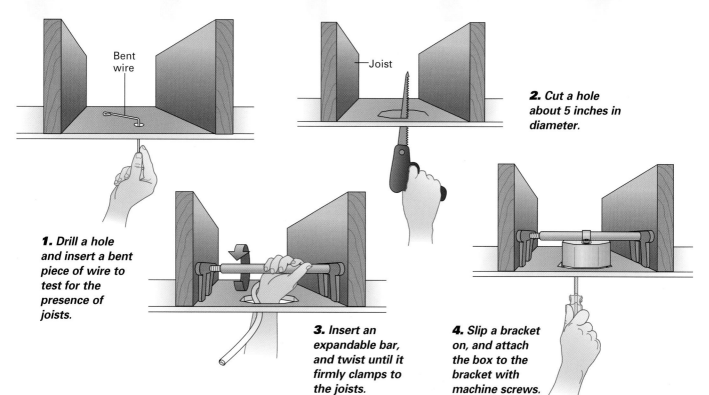

1. Drill a hole and insert a bent piece of wire to test for the presence of joists.

Bent wire

Joist

2. Cut a hole about 5 inches in diameter.

3. Insert an expandable bar, and twist until it firmly clamps to the joists.

4. Slip a bracket on, and attach the box to the bracket with machine screws.

keyhole saw. Attach 2×2 or 2×4 cleats on each joist so you will have a nailing surface for the wallboard patch later.

Cut a wallboard patch ¼ inch smaller than the cutout. Set the ceiling box on the patch in the position where it will be placed, trace, and cut out the box hole.

Run the cable, and clamp it to the box. Install the brace, screwing the bracket ends to the cleats. Slide the box into exact position.

Press the wallboard patch in place. Don't force it; take it down and trim it if necessary. Then anchor the patch with wallboard screws. Apply wallboard tape and several coats of joint compound, then sand, prime, and paint.

If you have a plaster ceiling, cut a channel and install a braced bar in the plaster ceiling (*see pages 44–45*).

EXPANDABLE BRACE BAR: This costs more than a standard braced box, but it can save you plenty of work.

Cut a hole slightly larger than the box. Run the cable. Adjust the bar so it is an inch or so shorter than the distance between the joists. Slip the bar into the hole, center it over the hole, and twist it until its ends clamp firmly to the joists. Run cable into the box and clamp it. Slip a bracket onto the bar, and fasten the box to the bracket with screws.

BRACE FROM ABOVE: If you have access to an unfinished attic above, you can install a box without damaging your ceiling. First cut the hole for the box. Attach a side-bracket box directly to a joist; or install a piece of 2×4 blocking between joists, and screw the box to it. For the strongest installation, do both.

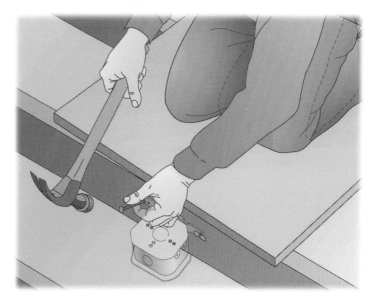

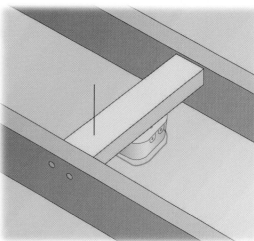

A side-bracket box attached to a joist with nails or screws will be strong, but not strong enough for a ceiling fan. Add bracing.

To mount a ceiling-fan box, install a piece of blocking between the joists and anchor the box to the blocking.

RUNNING CABLE IN FINISHED SPACES

Back-to-back boxes are easy to install. Cut a hole for the new box, and pull out the existing receptacle. Poke cable through if the distance is short, or use two fish tapes.

Don't be afraid to devise your own method for snaking cable through walls. However, always make sure the cable will be protected if someone later drives a nail into the wall. Avoid bending cable into tight turns—you can damage the wires.

For short runs, you can sometimes just thread the cable through. However, fish tapes make the job much easier (*see pages 60–61*). **BEHIND MOLDINGS:** Often you can minimize the arduous job of wall patching by running cable in cavities you cut behind moldings.

If the moldings are painted, cut the line between molding and wall with a utility knife, so you won't peel paint when you pry the molding off. Use a flat prybar, and work carefully to avoid denting the wood as you pull it off. Remove the finishing nails by grasping them with a pair of tongue-and-groove pliers and prying them out from the back side. Or, leave the nails in so you can carefully poke each one back into its original hole when you refasten the molding.

Drill through the studs, pull the cable, and protect it with metal plates wherever the cable is within 1¼ inches of the wall surface. Armored cable (BX) provides some added protection, but not insurance, against puncture by nails.

ABOVE CEILINGS, UNDER FLOORS: If at all possible, avoid running cable through wall studs in finished wall; the notching and patching involved will take far longer than the actual wiring. Instead, run cable through an attic, basement, or crawl space to a new box. If you can take this approach, the only difficult part of the job will be fishing cable through wall cavities.

RUNS ACROSS A WALL: If you have no alternative but to run cable across walls, you'll have to cut into wallboard or plaster, notch the studs, install the cable, and patch the wall. Because the cable will be close to the wall surface, you'll need to install protective metal plates before patching.

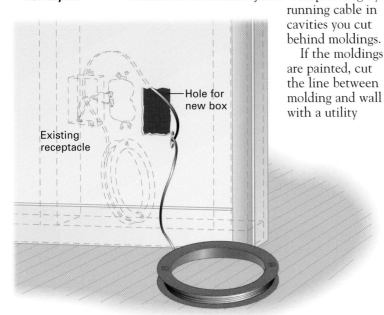

Hole for new box

Existing receptacle

To run cable around a doorway, remove the casing. Saw or whittle a little from each of the shims, and lay the cable in the space between the jamb and the frame. Install a protective plate where the cable must run across the shims.

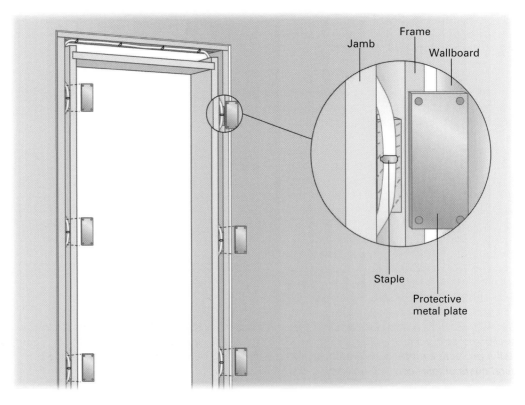

Jamb

Frame

Wallboard

Staple

Protective metal plate

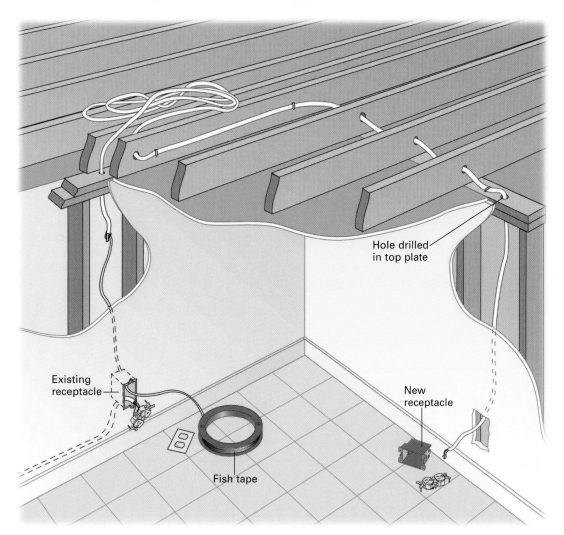

Run cable from an existing receptacle to a new ceiling box, wall switch, or receptacle by going up into the attic and back down.

Hole drilled in top plate

Existing receptacle

Fish tape

New receptacle

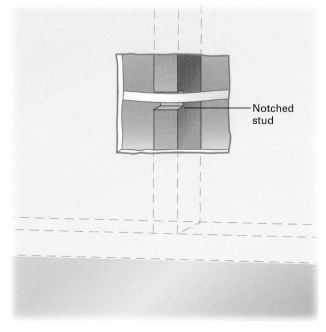

Notched stud

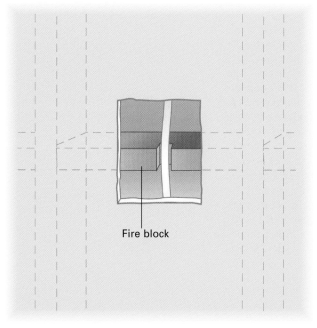

Fire block

To make a run across the wall, cut out a piece of plaster or wallboard about 5 inches square. Notch the stud, and install a protective metal plate. Patch, apply tape and several coats of joint compound, and sand smooth.

Some older homes have fire block—horizontal pieces spanning between the joists, about halfway up the wall. Notch and patch these as well.

RUNNING CABLE IN FINISHED SPACE
continued

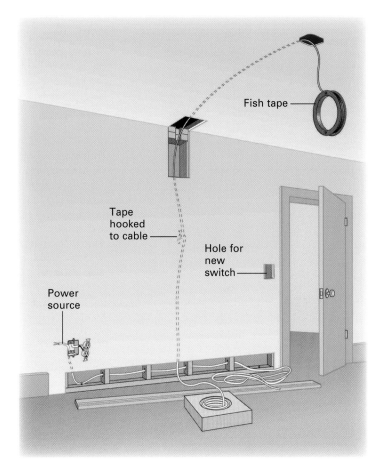

Fish tape

Tape hooked to cable

Hole for new switch

Power source

ADDING A NEW CEILING FIXTURE:

If you have no access from above, you'll have to cut a hole in the ceiling and the wall.

Cut a hole for a ceiling box in the center of the room (*see page 64*). If the joists run parallel to the wall with the switch, use a stud sensor to follow the joists on each side of the hole to the wall. Cut adjoining rectangular holes in the ceiling and upper wall, large enough to reach the cable. Use a keyhole saw, chisel, or reciprocating saw to cut a channel for the cable in the top plate.

Run a fish tape through the ceiling cavity to the cutout at the junction of the wall and ceiling; if the run is long, use two fish tapes (*see page 60*). Fish cable to the baseboard cutout, then to the switch. Install a protective metal plate at the top of the wall, and patch the holes.

If the path to the switch runs perpendicular to the joists, you will have to cut holes along the ceiling and notch the joists as shown on page 67. To avoid cutting and patching all those holes, it may make sense to run the cable parallel to the joists to another wall, then down behind the baseboard (and around doors), and over to the switch wall.

If you have an existing ceiling fixture that is controlled by a pull chain, you can wire it to a switch in the wall by running a single cable from the ceiling fixture to a box in the wall. Connect the wires as in the second option shown on page 79.

Grab power for a new ceiling fixture (above) from a receptacle in the same room. Run one cable to the switch, another to the ceiling box. If there is no fire block in the wall and if you can snake cable behind the baseboard or through a basement or crawl space, you will have only one area to patch. Install protective metal plates wherever nails might pierce the cable.

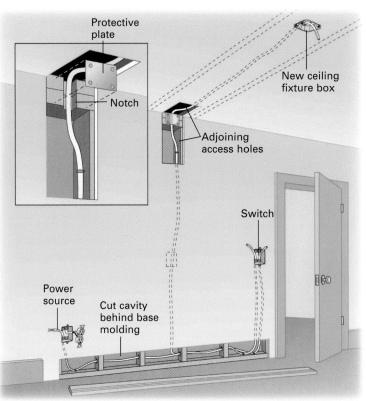

Protective plate

Notch

New ceiling fixture box

Adjoining access holes

Switch

Power source

Cut cavity behind base molding

A 16-inch-long cutout at the top of the wall will give you room to push the fish tape down into the cavity. Patching a cutout this size is not much more trouble than a smaller one. Run the fish tape from the ceiling box hole to the cutout and then down the wall.

RACEWAY WIRING

Surface-mounted wiring, also called raceway wiring, will save you from cutting, patching, and painting walls and ceilings. Raceway takes more work and money than conduit (which also can be mounted on a wall) but is less obtrusive-looking. Check your local codes before installing raceway; it may not be allowed in areas other than living rooms or bedrooms.

Some systems include a baseboard channel that can hide not only electrical wiring but also TV cable and telephone lines. You can install receptacles and jacks at various points in the baseboard.

There will be lots of parts to buy—elbows, tees, channels, and boxes. Make a drawing of your installation, and have a salesperson help you assemble all the pieces you need.

Shut off the power. Begin by installing a starter box over an existing receptacle box. Cut the channels using a hacksaw, and attach them to the wall with screws driven into studs. Run wires through the channels,

installing special clips to hold the wires in place. Make the electrical connections and test all components. Finally, snap or screw on covers for the channels and boxes.

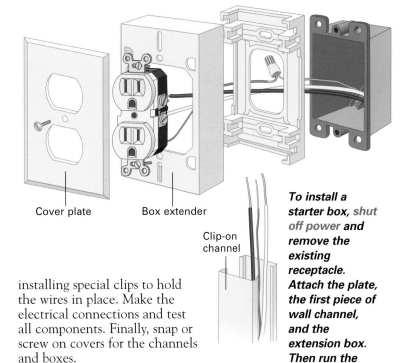

Cover plate   Box extender

Clip-on channel

To install a starter box, shut off power and remove the existing receptacle. Attach the plate, the first piece of wall channel, and the extension box. Then run the wiring.

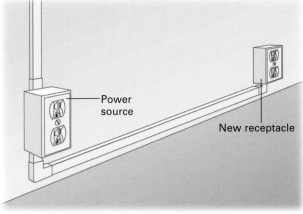

To install this system, first attach channels and boxes, then wires, then snap or screw on channel and receptacle covers.

Power source

New receptacle

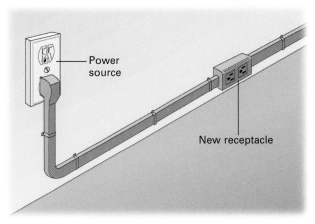

Power source

New receptacle

Flexible plug-in raceway is essentially a thick extension cord that you attach to the wall.

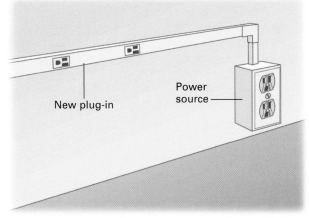

New plug-in

Power source

A raceway with built-in plug-ins is ideal for a workshop.

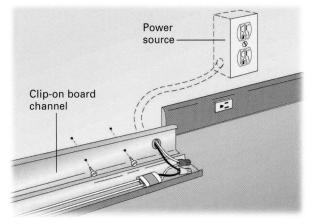

Power source

Clip-on board channel

Some baseboard raceway models carry telephone and TV cable as well as electrical wiring.

PLANNING NEW CIRCUITS

Though it may seem an imposing project, running new circuits actually does not call for skills beyond those needed for modest projects. Essentially, you must install the new receptacles, appliances, and/or lights; run cable from them into the service panel; and attach two wires, one to a new breaker and one to the neutral bar (*see pages 72–73 for instructions*). Chances are, the most demanding physical work will be patching walls after you have finished.

However, new circuits must be planned carefully. On these two pages we give some general guidelines for determining when to install a new circuit, as well as how to apportion the service. If you feel at all unsure, consult with a professional electrician or with your building department.

WORKING TO CODE

Building codes are inescapable when installing new circuits. If you upgrade without getting a permit, you may run into trouble when you sell your house. More importantly, your local building department provides a vital service, ensuring safety both during and after installation. Though it will seem bothersome, it is in your best interest to satisfy codes and your inspector.

VISIT THE BUILDING DEPARTMENT: Call or visit your building department to get a general idea of how you should proceed. Chances are, they will have some literature that provides guidelines for electrical work. Do not expect them to help you plan the work; their job is to inspect, not to assist. In some localities, they will require that all new circuits be installed by a licensed electrician.

MAKE A PLAN: Make a neat, written plan of the work you will perform. This should include a rough drawing and a complete list of materials to be used—sizes of wires and cables, make and type of breaker, make and type of boxes.

Bring the plan when you first meet with inspectors. It will help you demonstrate that you understand what needs to be done and

STANDARD CIRCUIT REQUIREMENTS

These are only general guidelines. Local codes may have very specific requirements.

Room	Requirements
Kitchen	Two 20-amp circuits for receptacles; they must serve the kitchen only. One 15-amp lighting circuit. An older microwave may need its own circuit. If, for example, you sometimes run a microwave, toaster, dishwasher, and coffee maker at the same time, be sure they are not all on the same circuit. An electric range requires its own 250-volt circuit.
Bathroom	A 20-amp circuit for the GFCI receptacle, to handle blow dryers. If you have an overhead heat lamp/fan/light, it will need its own 15- or 20-amp circuit.
Garage	One 15-amp circuit; if you use it as a shop, add circuits to handle your power tools.
Workshop	Add up the wattage of the tools you may use at one time. Based on this total, install one or two 20-amp circuits, plus a 15-amp light circuit.
Living room, dining room	One 15-amp general-purpose circuit per 500 square feet, for switches, lights, bedroom, hallway, and receptacles. You may need a separate 15-amp circuit for a home office. Install separate small-appliance circuits for air conditioners as needed.
Laundry	One 20-amp circuit for a washer and a gas dryer. A separate 250-volt circuit for an electric dryer.
Basement	A 15-amp circuit for lights and receptacles if the basement is finished. A separate 20-amp circuit for a water softener and sump pump. A separate 250-volt circuit for an electric water heater.

that you intend to do the job properly. Codes will require at least one inspection. Be clear about how the job should look when the inspector arrives on site; do not cover any wires or boxes that need to be seen.

DO YOU NEED A NEW CIRCUIT?

If you need to install only a few receptacles or lights, you may be able to tap into an existing circuit instead of installing a new one. Just be sure you do not overload the circuit.

SAFE CAPACITY: All the fixtures and appliances used by a circuit should add up to no more than a circuit's *safe capacity*, which is its total capacity minus 20 percent. A 15-amp circuit, for instance, has a maximum capacity of 1,800 watts (15 amps × 120 volts = 1,800 watts), and a safe capacity of 1,440 watts.

DO THE MATH: Calculate the wattage used by a circuit. Light bulbs and most appliances have the wattage printed on them. If only the amperage is shown, multiply the amperage by 120 volts. For instance, a microwave rated at 6 amps uses 720 watts.

Add all the wattage numbers to get the total load for the circuit, then compare that number to its safe capacity. Safe capacity for a 15-amp circuit is 1,440 watts; for a 20-amp circuit, 1,920 watts.

If a circuit can safely handle its current load plus the load of your new installations, just tap into it. If the total wattage exceeds safe capacity, you need a new circuit.

TOTAL SERVICE CAPACITY

Homeowners are sometimes perplexed to find that the total amperage of all their circuit breakers adds up to more than the rating of the service panel. For instance, a 100-amp service panel may have circuit breakers whose amperage adds up to more than 200 amps. This is not cause for alarm and it does not mean that you cannot add a circuit or two.

BUS BAR LIMITS: A service panel's amperage rating tells you not how much total amperage you can have, but how much amperage *each hot bar* can handle. So a 100-amp service panel can handle 200 amps of electrical use as long as the usage is balanced, with 100 watts on each bar.

In fact, it is not unusual for the breakers on a single bar to add up to more than the total service amperage. That is because all the circuits almost certainly will never be used to full capacity at any one time. If one of your hot bars carries more than the amperage rating, you may want to move a breaker or two to the other hot bar.

If either of the hot bars overloads, the main circuit breaker or fuse will trip or blow. This is

not dangerous; but if it happens often, you need new, larger service to the house.

OVERLOADS: In general, if a house is less than 3,500 square feet and does not have electric heat or unusual appliances, 100 amps should be plenty. However, if you have concerns about electrical usage, get a professional inspection. With 60-amp service, you may run into problems if you have air conditioners or other heavy-use appliances.

ADDING A SINGLE NEW CIRCUIT

If your kitchen appliances trip a breaker or blow a fuse more than once a month, and changing the plugs around doesn't solve the problem, you probably need a new circuit. Or, if you plan to put in a new appliance, such as an air conditioner, calculate the wattage use on your existing receptacle circuit to see whether you need a new circuit.

To divide one circuit into two, shut off the power and chart the course of the wires. If you encounter a junction box where two or more cables converge (preferably in the basement), you may be able to unsplice wires and hook several receptacles to a new circuit. If not, it is often easiest to connect the last two or three receptacles on a line to a new circuit. See pages 60–68 for tips on running new cable with minimal damage to walls. Or, run the new circuit outside, using conduit approved for exterior use. Drilling a couple of holes through the house and bending conduit (*see pages 56–57*) may be less work than cutting and patching walls.

ADDING SEVERAL CIRCUITS

If you are doing remodeling work, draw a plan that maps where all the circuits will go (*see pages 10–12*), and have your plan approved by your building department.

Use the chart (*opposite*) as a general guide. Place no more than 8 receptacles on a 15-amp general-purpose circuit; kitchens, bathrooms, and shop areas need 20-amp circuits with only a few receptacles per circuit. Add up the wattage of your lights to make sure a lighting circuit will not be overloaded. Wiring more than one circuit can get complicated, and a plan helps to see the wiring clearly. If you are building an addition, run the cables and have the work inspected before applying wallboard (*see pages 58–59*). If you are working on old walls, remove all the plaster or wallboard before you work.

Check your service panel to make sure there is enough space for all the new breakers you need (*see pages 72–73*).

ADDING NEW CIRCUITS

When adding or replacing a breaker, disable power by shutting off the main breaker. For total protection, shut off the main disconnect or have the utility company turn off the power.

When you are installing a new circuit, most of the work will be outside the service panel. Before you tap into the service panel, you will install boxes; run cable all the way to the service panel (electricians call this a "home run"); and connect switches, receptacles, or fixtures.

But before you begin any of this work, examine your service panel, check with the local building department to make sure you can install new circuits, and purchase the breakers that you will need.

Study pages 70–71 to tell whether you need new circuits and to make sure your electrical service can handle them.

"Skinny" breaker   Single-pole breaker

Double-pole breaker

then from the subpanel to the main panel. However, a better solution is to hire an electrician to install a completely new panel with breakers.

LOOK FOR BLANKS: If you have circuit breakers, look for blank spaces. Depending on the type of service panel you have, you may see unbroken knockouts, or there may be space on a hot bus bar where a new breaker can be attached.

NO MORE ROOM?: If all the spaces are taken, you may be able to replace a standard breaker with two "skinnies," which are half as thick. Before you do this, check to make sure skinnies are available for your service panel and your building department will allow you to install them yourself. If not, you may have to hire an electrician to install a new service panel with more spaces.

Main breaker

FINDING ROOM IN THE SERVICE PANEL

If you have a fuse box, it is usually not possible to connect a new circuit to it. Instead, you can install a subpanel, which is essentially an additional small service panel: Run cable for the new circuit to the subpanel,

DISCONNECT THE POWER

Shutting off the main breaker will de-energize the hot bus bars and all the breakers attached to them, but it will not shut off power to the wires that enter the service panel and connect to the main breaker.

SAFETY FIRST: Many electricians consider it perfectly safe to work in a service panel with the main breaker shut off; just make sure you do not touch those large wires coming in from the outside. For added safety, turn off power coming into the service panel by shutting off a main disconnect. Wear rubber-soled shoes and stand on a wooden platform. Codes may require you to completely de-energize the entire panel. Alert another member of the household you are beginning a serious electrical operation.

MAIN DISCONNECT: If you are fortunate, you will have a main disconnect that is separate from the service panel. It may be a box that looks like a small service panel

Most service boxes will have room for new breakers. The breakers will fit in knockout plugs on the front of the panel. New cable goes through knockout holes on the side.

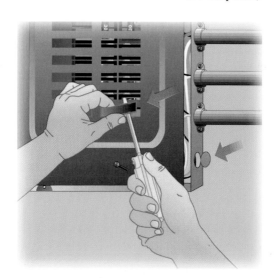

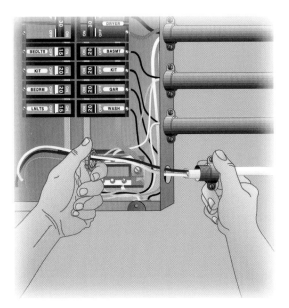

1. *Strip plenty of sheathing, punch out a knockout in the side of the panel, and clamp the cable.*

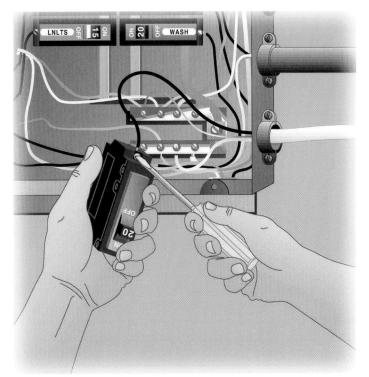

outside the house, just beyond the meter. Shut it off before working on your service panel.

If you have no main disconnect and you want to shut off all power to the panel, arrange for the power company to turn off power for a specific amount of time.

Use a voltmeter or neon tester to make sure that the power is off.

INSTALLING NEW BREAKERS

Remove the cover to expose the insides of the panel. There will be a mass of wires, perhaps tangled, running around the breakers. Take a few minutes to see where they all go. If one of the wires is not connected to a breaker, that means an old circuit has been discontinued; pull the wire out of the panel, or at least cap it off with a wire nut.

REMOVE SHEATHING: Strip enough sheathing from your new line so that the black or colored wire can reach the breaker and the white or neutral wire can reach an available terminal on the neutral bus bar. The wires must travel around the breakers.

KNOCKOUTS: Punch out a knockout in the side of the panel, and clamp the cable firmly to it just as you would clamp cable in a box. Strip ¾ inch of insulation from the wires. Carefully bend the wires so they will stay out of the way. Loosen a terminal screw on the neutral bar, insert the white wire into the hole, and tighten the screw; do the same with the ground wire, if any.

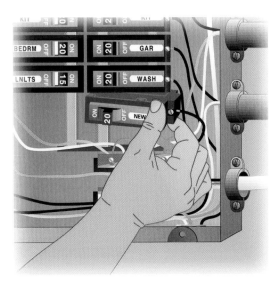

2. *Strip ¾" of insulation from the hot and neutral wire. Connect the neutral wire to the neutral bus bar, and the hot wire to the breaker.*

3. *To attach the breaker, slip one side over into place, and push the other firmly.*

WIRE AND INSTALL: Loosen the terminal screw on the breaker, insert the hot wire into the hole, and tighten the screw. Snap the breaker into place. Usually, this means sliding one side over so it engages, then pushing on the other side until it clamps firmly. The new breaker should be pressed as deeply into the panel as the surrounding breakers. Some 250-volt circuits, often called 125/250-volt circuits, have two hot wires running to the breaker and a white wire running to the neutral bar. Water heaters and other appliances have only two colored wires attached to the breaker, and a ground wire attached to the neutral bar. For instructions on installing a GFCI breaker, see page 38.

TELEPHONE AND CABLE WIRING

Running these cables is not difficult, and there is no danger of electrocution. But the connections must be secure and the wires must be protected against damage in order for your telephone, your TV, and your computer modem to run properly.

These lightweight cables often are run on top of or next to moldings, where they are visible. Your rooms will definitely have a neater appearance if the cables are hidden.

RG 6 Coaxial cable

Category 5 Phone cable

DO IT YOURSELF OR CONTRACT?

Before running wires for your telephone or cable TV service, check the cost of having the company do it for you. There are a number of variables to consider.

Having the phone company run lines may incur only a small expense. And all the cable installed by the company may be warrantied, meaning that future repairs will be free, while repairs to wires you installed may cost you plenty.

The cable TV company not only might charge you for running a new line, but they also may add a monthly charge for an additional TV hookup. (If you need a cable box for each TV, you will get this charge regardless of who runs the cable.)

Telephone and cable installers can quickly run fairly neat lines. But in most cases, the cables will be visible; company installers will not go to great lengths to hide cables. Before you hire a company to run cable inside your house, discuss exactly where the lines will run. You may decide to do it yourself just to get a neater appearance.

Of course, the cable or telephone company will run all exterior lines. Don't use interior jacks and splitters on the outside; they will corrode. If you will run interior lines yourself, negotiate with the cable or telephone line installers for the best possible point of entry into the house. If you ask, they may leave a roll of cable for interior lines.

Surface-mount telephone jacks are simple to install; use them even if you will hide the cable.

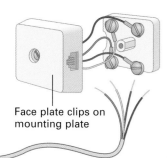

Face plate clips on mounting plate

Mounting plate

Face plate screws in place

Round, flush-mount jacks barely protrude from the wall.

Pull coaxial cable through a wall cavity and connect it to a wall jack.

Coaxial wall jack

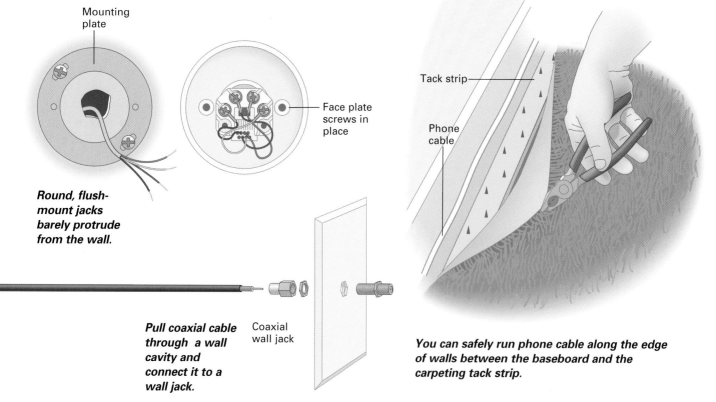

Tack strip

Phone cable

You can safely run phone cable along the edge of walls between the baseboard and the carpeting tack strip.

RUNNING CABLE

Choose high-quality cable, rather than cheaper versions. Purchase telephone cable that uses solid-core wire, labeled "24-AWG." Use "Category 3" for telephone use; "Category 5" for computer modem use.

Use "shielded" coaxial RG6 cable for TV, with a wrapping of metal under the insulation (avoid the RG59 cable sold at many home centers—your cable company may refuse to hook up to it). Shielded cable makes surer connections than nonshielded cable does.

PLAN FIRST: Plan the cable path carefully to avoid hazardous situations. For instance, you cannot run a cable across a doorway on top of a hardwood floor. You may be able to avoid this by drilling a small hole and poking the cable through a wall.

HIDE THE CABLE: To hide cable under wall-to-wall carpeting, lift up one section of carpet at a time with a pair of lineman's pliers, and position the cable between the tack strip and the base molding. Push the carpet firmly back into place.

If you choose to hide cable behind molding, be sure there is space behind the molding so you do not end up squashing the cable. If the molding is painted, use a knife to cut through the paint where the molding meets the wall; otherwise, paint will crack when you pull the molding off. Use a flat prybar to avoid marring the wood. Replace the moldings by reinserting the nails and tapping with a scrap of wood to prevent dents.

Use rounded staples to attach cable to walls; standard rectangular staples may bite into wire insulation.

INSTALLING JACKS

Surface-mounted jacks are simple to install. Attach the plate to the wall with a screw. Strip wire ends and connect them to terminals, and attach the cover with a screw.

To install a telephone wall jack, cut a hole in the wall for a standard old-work electrical box (see pages 62–63). Directly below, drill a small hole near the floor. Attach a small weight to a string, and let it down through the wall cavity. Stick a piece of bent wire into the bottom hole, grab the string, and pull it out. Now you can use the string to pull cable up through the wall. Install the box in the wall, and attach a phone jack to the box.

To attach coaxial cable to a connector or jack, strip ¾ inch of insulation down to the wire, then ⅜ inch of outer insulation, taking care not to damage the thin metal shielding. When you screw on the connector, it will grab the shielding as well as the insulation.

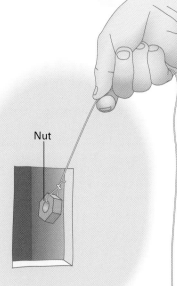

Nut

1. *To install a telephone wall jack, cut a hole for a standard electrical box. Tie a small weight (a nut or washer, for example—the smaller, the better) to a string, and lower it down through the wall.*

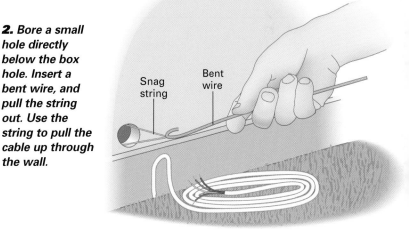

Snag string   Bent wire

2. *Bore a small hole directly below the box hole. Insert a bent wire, and pull the string out. Use the string to pull the cable up through the wall.*

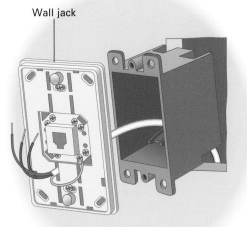

Wall jack

3. *Run the cable into the box, and clamp it. Attach the box to the wall. Strip sheathing and wire insulation, and connect the wire ends to the terminals on a wall jack. Attach the jack to the box with screws.*

ADDING NEW FIXTURES

Once you've learned basic splicing skills as well as how to run cable and install boxes, you're ready to install just about any electrical fixture in your home. All that's needed is to figure out which wire goes where. This chapter shows you how to add receptacles and a variety of lights, with an emphasis on wiring configurations.

For most of us, wiring is a mind bender. Don't be surprised to find yourself returning to the diagrams again and again as you work on your project.

Electricity moves in a loop (thus the term "circuit"), so running power is a simple matter of providing a hot wire that goes to the fixture and a neutral wire coming back; a switch provides a break in the hot line that can be opened and closed.

But there's a lot more to household electricity than ON and OFF. Perhaps you want to control more than one light with a single switch, or control a light with two or even three switches; or have a switch that controls part of a receptacle. All of these situations call for specific wiring configurations. In this chapter you'll learn to make installations every bit as sophisticated as those made by the pros.

In addition, you'll find some common projects to enhance your home's comfort and beauty: recessed canister lights, fans to vent a bathroom or circulate air throughout the house, and outside receptacles and lights.

After decades of neglect, wall sconces have come back into fashion. Use them where muted, indirect lighting is called for. Place a wall sconce just above eye height so it will provide a pleasant upward accent and not glare.

PUTTING IT ALL TOGETHER

The projects in this chapter call for skills covered earlier in this book. Refer to these pages:

- Installing boxes   62–65
- Running cable   54–61, 66–68
- Adding new circuits   70–73
- Attaching wires   25–27
- Installing ceiling fixtures 41–45

IN THIS CHAPTER

Adding New Receptacles **78**

Ceiling Fixture with Switch **79**

Two Fixtures on One Switch **80**

Fixtures on Separate Switches **81**

Three-Way, Power to Switch, Fixture, Switch **82**

Three-Way, Power to Fixture, Switch, Switch **83**

Three-Way, Power to Switch, Switch, Fixture **84**

Three-Way with Receptacle: Four-Way **85**

Recessed Lights **86**

Bathroom Vent Fan **88**

Whole-House Fan **89**

Attic Fan **90**

Back-to-Back Outdoor Box **92**

Permanent Outdoor Fixtures **93**

ADDING NEW RECEPTACLES

You can use three-wire cable to wire receptacles on two different circuits. Attach the black wire to one breaker and the red to another. Both circuits use the same neutral wire.

The easiest way to install a new receptacle is to tap into an existing one. First, make sure the circuit can handle the extra load (*see page 70*). If you need several receptacles or if all your existing receptacles are maxed out, you'll have to install a new circuit.

TAPPING IN: It is easiest to tap into an end-of-the-line receptacle because it will have two terminals available. If you have to tap into a middle-of-the-run receptacle, use pigtails to make the connections, rather than attaching two wires to each terminal (*see page 34*). Shut off power and test that the circuit is dead. See that the box has room to accommodate two new wires. Run the cable and make the connections at both boxes

ON A NEW CIRCUIT: See pages 70–73 for how to run a new circuit. The illustration (*below left*) shows a

variation—using three-wire cable to install receptacles on two different circuits. Connect the red wire (hot for one circuit) to one breaker and the black (hot for the second circuit) to another. Connect some receptacles to the black-wire circuit, and some to the red-wire circuit. This configuration allows you to put a receptacle on another circuit later, in case one circuit becomes overloaded.

250-VOLT RECEPTACLES: A 250-volt receptacle must serve one appliance only. Install a breaker that is the correct size for your appliance, and run wires to match the breaker capacity (*see the chart on page 20*). To serve a 50-amp kitchen range, for example, install a 50-amp breaker and No. 6 wire; for a 30-amp dryer, install a 30-amp breaker and No. 10 wire. Receptacles have hole patterns based on amperage; make sure your appliance will plug into your receptacle.

Install a standard electrical box in the wall, or a flush-mounted box. Some codes require a double-wide box. A floor-mounted receptacle needs no box; attach it firmly to the floor.

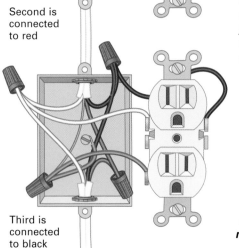

Power source —

First receptacle is connected to black

Second is connected to red

Third is connected to black

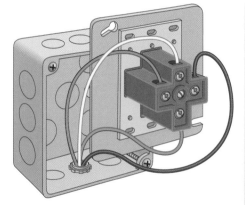

Use a two-gang receptacle box or a square junction box to wire a 250-volt wall receptacle.

CAUTION: HIGH VOLTAGE

Take special precautions when installing a 250-volt receptacle. With twice the power of a standard receptacle, it can seriously injure or even kill an adult. Make sure the power is off whenever installing or repairing.

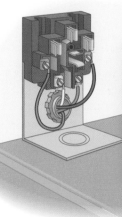

Receptacle cover

A floor receptacle for a 250-amp appliance needs no electrical box.

CEILING FIXTURE WITH SWITCH

When running cable for a switched ceiling fixture, send the power either into the switch box or into the fixture box—whichever is easier. Wiring is only slightly more difficult with power coming into the fixture. Test to see that power is off before beginning.

See pages 54–68 for instructions on running cable and installing boxes. Take power from a nearby receptacle or junction box, but only if doing so will not overload the circuit.

POWER TO SWITCH: Install cable into the boxes, and strip the ends off all the insulated wires. At the switch box, connect both black wires to the switch (it doesn't matter which wire goes to which terminal), and splice the two white wires with a wire nut. Tie the ground wires together, and attach a ground to the box if required.

At the fixture box, connect black wire to black lead and white wire to white lead. Connect the ground wire to the box or to the fixture if required.

POWER TO FIXTURE: Install cable and boxes, and strip the ends of all the insulated wires. At the switch box, use a marker to paint the end of the white wire black (it becomes the hot wire between the switch and fixture), and connect both the black and the painted wires to the switch. Tie the ground wires together.

At the fixture box, paint black the end of the white wire going to the switch. Connect the black wire from the power source to the painted wire. Connect the fixture's black lead to the black wire going to the switch, and the white lead to the white wire coming from the power source. Tie the ground wires together, and connect a ground wire to the fixture or to the box.

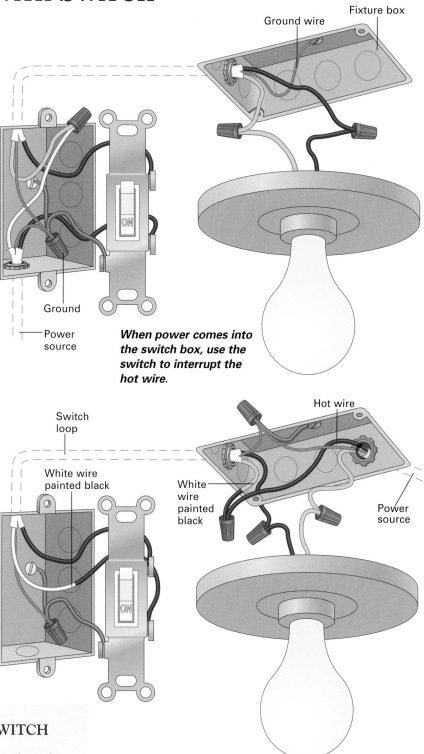

When power comes into the switch box, use the switch to interrupt the hot wire.

If power enters the fixture box first, continue the hot wire to the switch with a white wire that is painted black. The black wire travels from the switch back to the fixture, completing the loop.

HOT WIRES ONLY TO SWITCH

Never connect the white neutral wire directly to the switch; always connect it to the fixture. Otherwise, the light will work, but every time the switch is turned on there will be a dangerous potential for shock at the fixture because the neutral wire can no longer provide an unbroken path back to the service panel.

Both wires connected to the switch must be hot. If a white wire is used as a hot wire, paint it black at both ends to show that it is hot.

TWO FIXTURES ON ONE SWITCH

If you want two fixtures to come on when you flip one switch, it is easiest to have the power enter the switch, then travel to the first fixture and on to the second. You can connect as many lights as you want this way. It is common to connect a number of recessed canister lights (*see pages 86–87*) with this arrangement. The wiring is the same as for the "power to switch" option shown on page 79, with additional cable running from the first fixture to subsequent fixtures.

If you will be installing quite a few fixtures, add up the total wattage of all the bulbs and make sure the circuit can handle the load (*see page 70*).

See pages 54–68 for instructions on running cable and installing boxes. Take power from a receptacle or junction box, as long as doing so will not overload the circuit.

Shut off the circuit and test to see that power is off.

Run cable from the power source into the switch box, then from the switch box into the fixture box, then on to the next fixture box, and so on. Strip about ¾ inch of insulation from the wire ends.

At the switch box, connect the black wires to the switch terminals. (Note: It doesn't matter which wire goes to which terminal.) Connect the two white wires. Then tie the ground wires together, and attach them to the box if required.

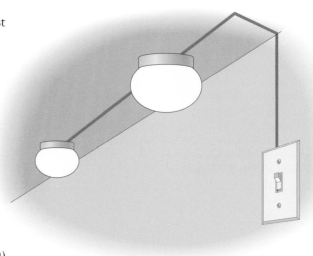

One switch controls as many fixtures as you like. Bring power to the switch box. Run two-wire cable from the switch to the first fixture, then to the second, and so on.

At the first fixture box, tie the two black wires to the fixture's black lead; tie the two white wires to the fixture's white lead. Tie the ground wires together, and fasten them to the fixture if required. If you have more than two fixtures, make the same connections for all but the last fixture. At the last fixture box, connect the black wire to the black lead and the white wire to the white lead. Connect the ground wire to the fixture or box if required.

To control multiple fixtures from a single switch, pass the hot wire through the switch, then to the fixtures. Connect all the white wires together in each box.

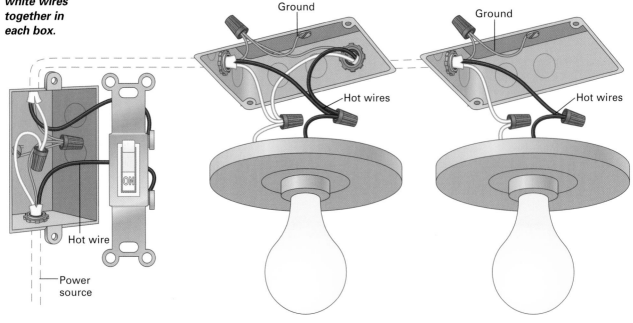

Ground

Ground

Hot wires

Hot wires

Hot wire

Power source

FIXTURES ON SEPARATE SWITCHES

Professional electricians often save in materials and labor by using three-wire cable to connect two separate installations. Because all neutral wires go back to the same neutral bar in the service panel, more than one fixture or switch can hitch a ride on any available neutral wire. This installation is one example of how you can sometimes run one three-wire cable instead of two two-wire cables.

See pages 54–68 for instructions on running cable and installing boxes. Take power from a nearby receptacle or junction box, as long as doing so will not overload the circuit.

Install two ceiling boxes and a two-gang switch box. Run two-wire cable from the power source to the far fixture box; run three-wire cable from the far fixture box to the near fixture box, and from the near fixture box back to the switch box. Strip all wire ends. Check that power is shut off to the circuit.

At the far fixture box, connect the black wires. Tie the two white wires to the white lead on the fixture and connect the red wire to the fixture's black lead. Tie together the ground wires, and connect to the fixture or box if required.

At the near fixture box, connect the two red wires and the two black wires. Paint the white wire coming from the switch box black—it's the hot wire. Connect the white painted wire to the fixture's black lead, and

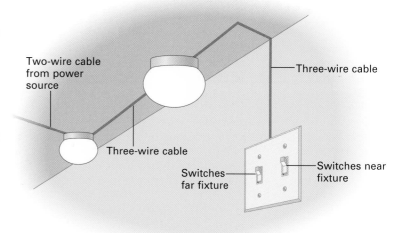

the white unpainted wire to the fixture's white lead. Tie together all the ground wires, and connect to the box or fixture if required.

At the switch box, tie two pigtails (short lengths of wire with each end stripped) to the black wire. Paint the white wire black to show that it is hot. Connect the red wire and a black pigtail to one switch; this will control the far fixture. Connect the white painted wire and the other black pigtail to the other switch; this will control the near fixture.

Each of the two side-by-side switches controls one fixture. Bring power into the far fixture box. Run three-wire cable between the fixtures and into the switch.

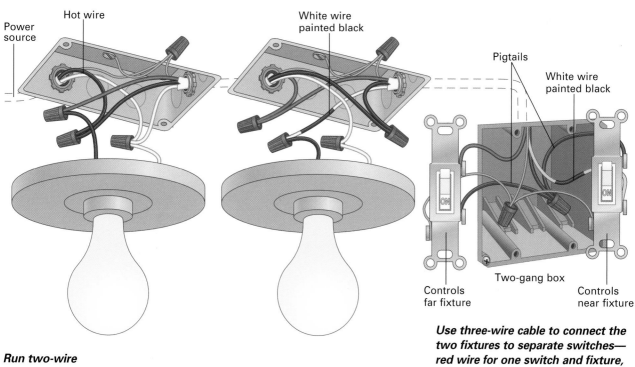

Run two-wire cable from the power source to the first fixture.

Use three-wire cable to connect the two fixtures to separate switches— red wire for one switch and fixture, black wire for the other switch and fixture. Tie together all the neutral and ground wires.

THREE-WAY, POWER TO SWITCH, FIXTURE, SWITCH

Two switches can control the same fixture. Bring power to the first switch. Run three-wire cable from the first switch to the fixture and from the fixture to the second switch.

Use two three-way switches to control a single fixture (or a series of fixtures tied together) from two locations. In the next few pages you'll find three options for wiring three-ways, depending on your power source. Three-ways are complicated; follow the diagrams closely.

See pages 54–68 for instructions on running cable and installing boxes. Take power from a nearby receptacle or junction box, as long as doing so will not overload the circuit.

When wiring three-ways, no matter the direction of power, always connect the hot wire from the power source to the common terminal of one switch; run a wire from the second switch's common terminal to the fixture's black wire; and run traveler wires from switch to switch, never to the fixture.

See that power to the circuit is off. Run two-wire cable from the power source to the first switch box. Run three-wire cable from the first switch box to the fixture and from the fixture to the second switch box. Strip about ¾ inch of insulation from the ends of all wires. Tie all the ground wires together, and attach the ground to the boxes, switches, or fixture if required.

At the first switch box, attach the hot wire from the power source to the switch's common terminal. Connect the white wires together. Attach the red and black wires leading to the fixture to the traveler terminals of the switch.

At the fixture, paint the white wire from the second switch black. Connect the red wires together; connect the black wire from the first switch to the painted white wire. Connect the black wire from the second switch to the fixture's black lead, and the white wire from the first switch to the fixture's white lead.

At the second switch, paint the white wire black. Attach the black wire to the common terminal. Attach the other two wires to the other terminals.

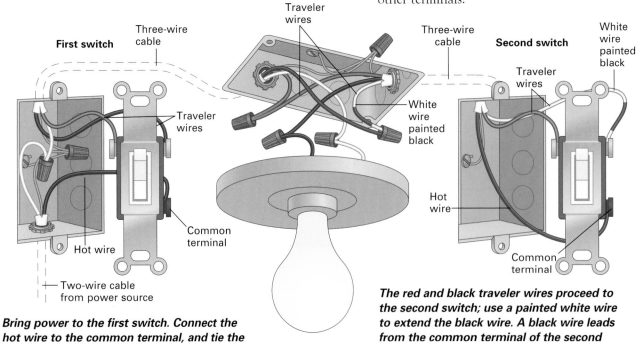

First switch — Three-wire cable — Traveler wires — Traveler wires — Common terminal — Hot wire — Two-wire cable from power source

Bring power to the first switch. Connect the hot wire to the common terminal, and tie the white wires together.

White wire painted black — White wire painted black — Three-wire cable — **Second switch** — Traveler wires — White wire painted black — Hot wire — Common terminal

The red and black traveler wires proceed to the second switch; use a painted white wire to extend the black wire. A black wire leads from the common terminal of the second switch to the fixture's black lead; connect the white lead to the white wire.

THREE-WAY, POWER TO FIXTURE, SWITCH, SWITCH

Here, power enters the fixture and then moves on to the two switches. Use three-wire cable to connect only the two switches, and two-wire elsewhere.

See pages 54–68 for instructions on running cable and installing boxes. Take power from a nearby receptacle or junction box, as long as doing so will not overload the circuit.

When wiring three-ways, no matter the direction of power, always connect the hot wire from the power source to the common terminal of one switch; run a wire from the second switch's common terminal to the fixture's black wire; and run traveler wires from switch to switch, never to the fixture.

Test to see that power to the circuit is off. Run two-wire cable into the fixture box and from the fixture box to the first switch box. Strip the ends of all wires about ¾ inch. Tie all the ground wires together, and attach to the boxes, switches, or fixture if required.

At the fixture box, paint the white wire from the first switch black. Connect the black wires. Connect the white wire to the fixture's white lead, and the white painted wire to the fixture's black lead.

At the first switch box, paint both white wires black. Attach the painted white wire from the second switch and the red wire to the traveler terminals; attach the black wire from the fixture to the common terminal.

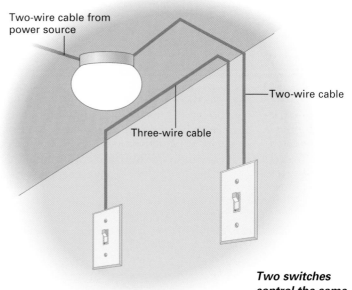

Connect the other remaining black and white painted wires together.

At the second switch box, paint the white wire black. Attach the white painted wire and the red wire to the traveler terminals; attach the black wire to the common terminal.

Two switches control the same fixture. Bring power to the fixture. Run two-wire cable from the fixture to the first switch; run three-wire cable from the first switch to the second switch.

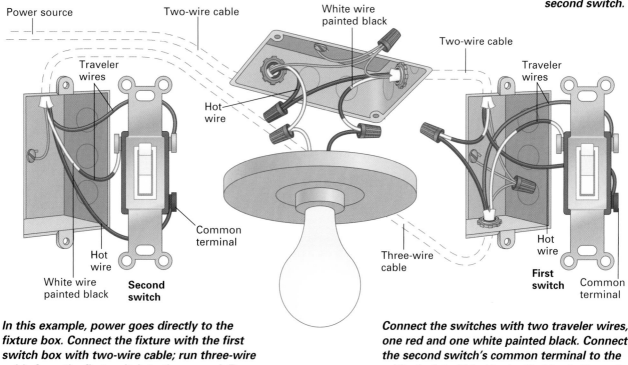

In this example, power goes directly to the fixture box. Connect the fixture with the first switch box with two-wire cable; run three-wire cable from the first switch to the second. Run the hot wire through to the first switch's common terminal, and attach the white wire to the fixture's white lead.

Connect the switches with two traveler wires, one red and one white painted black. Connect the second switch's common terminal to the white (painted black) wire that leads through the first switch's box and on to the fixture's black lead.

THREE-WAY, POWER TO SWITCH, SWITCH, FIXTURE

The simplest way to install a light with two three-way switches is to connect the switches to each other with traveler wires, and run two-wire cable to the fixture.

See pages 54–68 for instructions on running cable and installing boxes. Take power from a nearby receptacle or junction box, as long as doing so will not overload the circuit.

When wiring three-ways, no matter the direction of power, always connect the hot wire from the power source to the common terminal of one switch; run a wire from the second switch's common terminal to the fixture's black wire; and run traveler wires from switch to switch, never to the fixture.

Check that power to the circuit is off.

Run power to the first switch using two-wire cable. Run three-wire cable from switch to switch, and two-wire cable from the second switch to the fixture. Tie all the ground wires together, and attach to the boxes, switches, or fixture if required.

At the first switch box, attach the hot wire to the common terminal, and connect the two white wires. Attach the red and black wires to the traveler terminals. At the second switch box, connect the red and black wires from the first switch to the second switch's traveler terminals; attach the black wire from the fixture to the common terminal. Connect the two white wires. At the fixture box, connect the two wires to the fixture's leads.

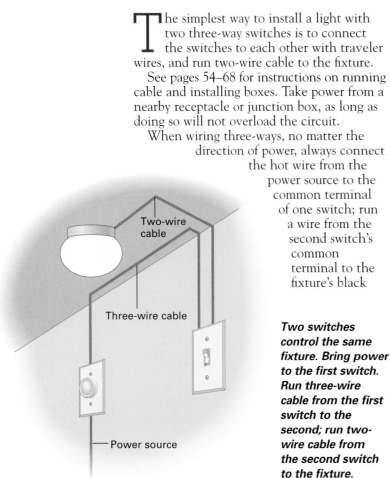

Two switches control the same fixture. Bring power to the first switch. Run three-wire cable from the first switch to the second; run two-wire cable from the second switch to the fixture.

THREE-WAY DIMMER

Install one three-way dimmer only; if you install a dimmer for both switches, they will burn out quickly. If you wire a three-way dimmer incorrectly, it will burn out as soon as power is turned on. Test with a three-way switch first.

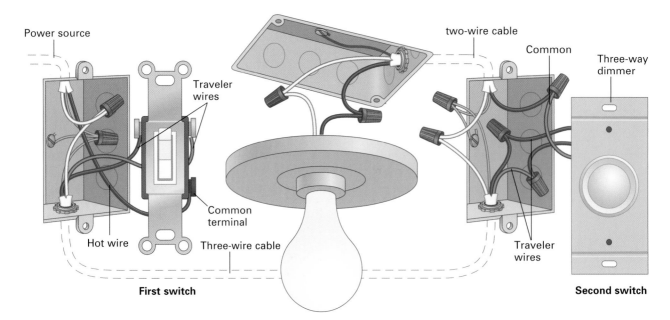

Bring power to the first switch box. Run three-wire cable from switch to switch, and two-wire cable from the second switch to the fixture. Attach the hot wire to the first switch's common terminal. Connect the two switches with black and red traveler wires. Attach the white wires in both switch boxes. Connect the wires in the fixture box to the fixture's leads.

THREE-WAY WITH RECEPTACLE: FOUR-WAY

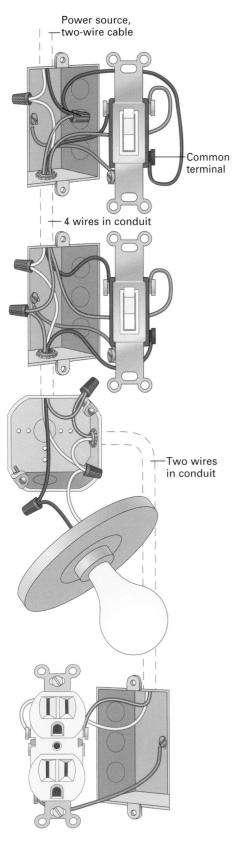

Power source, two-wire cable

Common terminal

4 wires in conduit

Two wires in conduit

This arrangement provides a receptacle that is always hot and a fixture controlled by two switches.

This is as complicated as household wiring gets. A four-way arrangement (*shown far right*) allows you to control a single fixture from three locations. To install three-way switches plus a receptacle, see the diagram (*right*).

See pages 54–68 for instructions on running cable and installing boxes. Take power from a nearby receptacle or junction box, as long as doing so will not overload the circuit. Check that power is shut off to the circuit before wiring.

The wiring schemes shown here use conduit as a ground. If you are using standard cable, add ground wires running through.

THREE-WAY WITH RECEPTACLE

Run power to the first switch; four wires to the second switch; three wires to the fixture; and two wires to the receptacle. Follow the diagram carefully. Tie the blue wire to the hot wire, and carry it through to the receptacle. The three-way wiring is the same as that shown (*opposite*).

FOUR-WAY

Install three-way switches at each end of the wiring, and as many four-ways in between as you like. Here the power comes into the fixture, but you can use the wiring routes shown on pages 82 and 84 as well.

Bring power into the fixture. From the fixture, branch out in two directions, running three wires to the first three-way switch and three wires to the four-way switch. Run three wires from the four-way switch to the second three-way switch.

Connect the hot wire to the first three-way's common terminal. Run traveler wires from switch to switch to switch. Connect four traveler wires— no hot wire—to the four-way switch. Follow the diagram closely for the other connections.

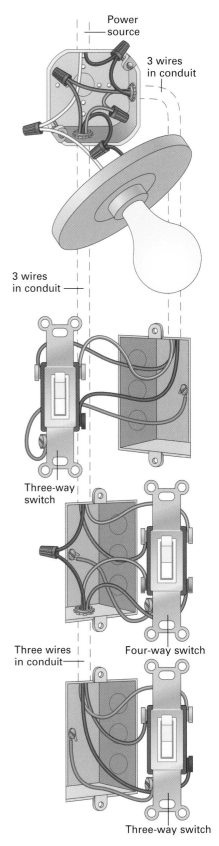

Power source

3 wires in conduit

3 wires in conduit

Three-way switch

Three wires in conduit

Four-way switch

Three-way switch

Use two three-way switches and one four-way switch to control a fixture from three locations.

RECESSED LIGHTS

Canister lights are recessed into the ceiling so that they are nearly flush with the ceiling surface. This makes them so unobtrusive and style-neutral that they are suitable for both new and old homes.

CHOOSING FIXTURES

Recessed lights typically use bulbs that are 75 watts or less. Because they point mostly down and not to the sides, brighter bulbs would not be of much use in illuminating a large room. If you need lots of light, install a number of recessed canisters.

SIZE: Make sure the lights will fit inside the ceiling. If your ceiling joists are 2×8s or smaller, you will need a specially sized box.

MOUNTING SYSTEM: If the ceiling is unfinished, or if you have access from above, use a fixture with telescoping brackets that attach to the joists. If the ceilings are finished and you have no access from above, buy old-work fixtures (*see below*) that clip into the ceiling. The lights do not weigh much, so this mounting method is strong enough. Use 5-inch canisters for small rooms, and 7-inch for larger rooms.

New-work canister with telescoping brackets fits between joists in new construction before wallboard goes up.

TRIMS AND CONES: Some recessed canisters are complete with a built-in trim piece. More commonly, you'll buy the canisters and the trims separately. Be sure the trim is the same size and make as the canister. Often, the trim costs more than the canister.

A basic trim is simply a ring that covers the gap between the ceiling material and the canister; because there is no lens, a floodlight is used. Or choose a trim with a lens, which allows you to use a standard light bulb. (Flood bulbs burn out more quickly than standard bulbs, so a trim with a lens will save you money in the long run.)

An eyeball trim swivels so you can point it in any direction to highlight a part of the room or a spot on the wall. Use it with a spotlight bulb, which produces a narrower shaft of light than a flood bulb.

Some trims also are cones that fit inside the canister. A black cone produces a subtle, diffused light; a silver reflecting cone intensifies the light. Use reflector flood bulbs with cones.

Install old-work canisters in a finished ceiling. Cut a hole between joists, run new cable, and make connections in the junction box. The clips hold the fixture in the hole.

Customize the appearance of your lights as well as the way they cast light by choosing from a variety of trim options.

Trim with lens to cover a standard light bulb

Adjustable eyeball trim

Reflector cone to intensify light

PREPARING FOR CANISTERS

You do not need to install boxes for canister fixtures; each has its own electrical box. See pages 54–68 for instructions on running cable.

CUT THE HOLES: If you will be installing a series of lights, map out the locations on graph paper. Use a compass to draw circles indicating the area to be lit by each canister, and position the lights so the circles overlap consistently.

However, you will probably not be able to put the lights exactly where you want them. Chances are good that a joist will be in the way; never cut a joist to make room for a canister. To do so can ruin the structural integrity of the ceiling.

Use an electronic stud sensor to find the joists, or drill a small hole and explore with a bent piece of wire (*see page 62*). Be sure that you have plenty of room for the canister before cutting the hole.

Use the template provided with the canister to draw a circle, and cut it with a keyhole saw or saber saw. Cut the circle precisely, because the trim will cover only about ¾ inch of gap.

Run cable to each hole; have a foot or so of extra cable to make installation easier. Strip sheathing and wire insulation.

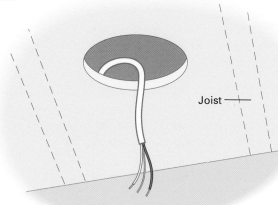

1. Cut the hole carefully so the canister will fit tightly. Run cable, and connect it to the canister's electrical box.

Joist

INSTALLING THE CANISTERS

The most common old-work canister uses four clips to clasp the canister to the wallboard or to the plaster and lath.

MAKE ELECTRICAL CONNECTIONS: Clamp cable to the junction box that is attached to the canister, and connect the wires to the fixture leads. If you are installing more than one fixture, run one cable in and one out, and connect wires as shown on page 80.

CLAMP THE CANISTER: Maneuver the cables and the junction box up into the hole. Push the canister all the way up so it is flush with the ceiling surface. With your fingers or a screwdriver, push up on each clip until it snaps into place, clipping the canister tightly to the drywall or plaster.

INSTALL TRIM AND BULB: Trims and cones usually connect to the canister with springs that you insert into holes in the canister. Make sure the trim is flush to the ceiling and centered around the canister. Screw in the light bulb and test.

2. Push the canister up tight against the ceiling, and push on each of the four clips until they clamp down tight. Install the trim and the light bulb.

Telescoping brackets

Junction box

Insulation

If the ceiling is not finished or if you have access from above, install a canister with telescoping brackets. Once in place, you can slide the canister to position it exactly.

BATHROOM VENT FAN

Bathrooms need ventilation to get rid of moisture and odors. The surest way to accomplish this is to install a vent fan. A fan or fan/light fixture takes up no more room than a light fixture. Wire it so you can control the fan and light separately, unless your local codes require that the fan come on whenever the light is on.

RUN DUCTING: For maximum efficiency, choose the most direct route possible for the ductwork. If you vent through the roof, install a flanged roof jack that will not leak.

If you live in an area with a cold climate, you'll save energy costs by buying a vent cap that closes snugly when not in use. Otherwise, cold air will have a path into your bathroom.

INSTALL THE FAN: Cut an opening between joists for the fan/light. Attach the fan directly to a joist using screws; make the bottom of the fan housing flush with the ceiling surface. Connect the ducting to the fan.

WIRE THE FAN AND SWITCH: Shut off power to the circuit. Use existing wiring, or run cable to the switch box and the ceiling box. To control the fan and the light separately, run three-wire cable from the switch to the fixture (*see page 81*). You may choose to use a one-gang box and a double switch (*see page 22*).

Restore power, test, and install the grille. Once or twice a year, clean the grille and the fan blades, and vacuum the area around the motor.

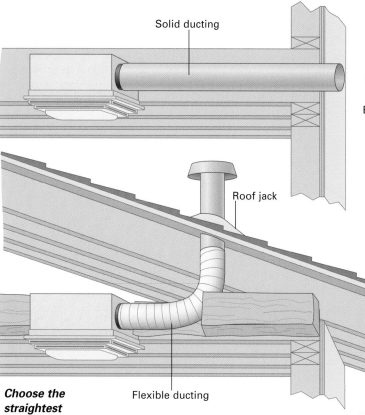

Solid ducting

End cap

Roof jack

Flexible ducting

Choose the straightest possible path for your ductwork. It is easiest to vent out through a wall. If you must vent through the roof, install an approved roof jack that will not leak.

MAKE SURE IT WILL VENT

Many bathroom vent fans pull little moisture out of the room, either because the ductwork is not efficient or because the fan motor is not powerful enough. Tell your supplier how large your bathroom is and how far the vent will have to travel, so you can get the right fixture and ducting. The more turns ductwork makes, the less efficient the fan will be. Solid ducts are more efficient than flexible ducts. Buy the most powerful fan you can afford.

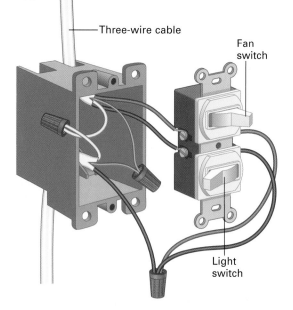

Three-wire cable

Fan switch

Light switch

Run power into the switch box. Use 3-wire cable to control the fan and the light with separate switches.

WHOLE-HOUSE FAN

By drawing air in through windows on the lower floors and out through the attic, a whole-house fan can save you plenty in air-conditioning costs. Some models come with a thermostat that turns the fan on when needed; others can be controlled with a two-speed, variable-speed timer, or an override switch. Note: These units must have adequate attic vents for exhausting the hot air. You may have to install larger or additional gable or roof vents.

CUT THE HOLE: In the ceiling of a top-floor hall, locate joists with a stud sensor. Remove any insulation from the area where you'll cut

the hole. Cut a hole for the fan in the plaster or wallboard only.

ATTACH THE FAN: Place the fan on top of the joists, centered over the hole. Fasten it with screws so it will not vibrate. Cut and install plastic or wood baffles to seal the spaces between the joists (many fans come with these).

MAKE ELECTRICAL CONNECTIONS: Shut off power to the circuit. Bring power to a switch box, and run cable to the fan or the fan thermostat. Install the switch. Restore power and test.

ATTACH THE LOUVER PANEL: Hold the louver panel in place so it covers the hole, and attach it by driving screws into joists.

2. Set the fan in place on top of the joists, and fasten it with screws. Fit the plastic baffles between the joists. Run cable into a switch box, then to the fan, and make electrical connections.

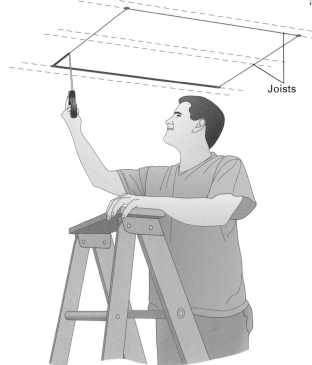

1. Prepare the area with a drop cloth—this is a messy job. Cut a hole in the ceiling drywall or plaster. Do not cut a joist.

Joists

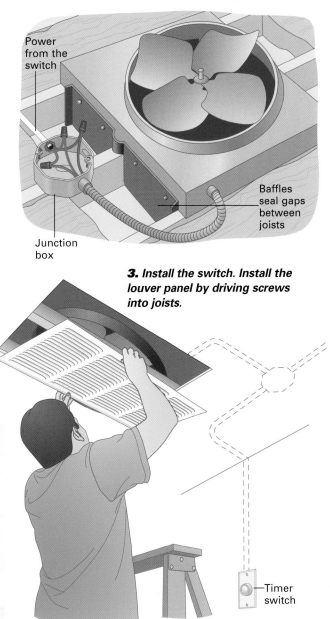

Power from the switch

Junction box

Baffles seal gaps between joists

3. Install the switch. Install the louver panel by driving screws into joists.

Timer switch

THE RIGHT SIZE

Decide whether you want the fan to pull air through the entire house, or whether you need only to ventilate a few rooms. For a fan to move air throughout the house, its CFM (cubic feet per minute) rating should be at least 3 times the total square footage of your house. Printed information that comes with the fan may tell you how large a house it can ventilate. Most whole-house fans have at least two speeds, so if a fan is too powerful, simply turn it down.

ATTIC FAN

An attic becomes intensely hot after a day of summer temperatures. When the attic is hot, the rest of the house will have a difficult time cooling off. Standard roof ventilators do not draw hot air out fast enough. An attic fan, however, will suck the hot air out quickly.

CHOOSING A FAN

SIZE: As a general rule, an attic fan's CFM (cubic feet per minute) rating should be nearly the same as the square footage of your attic. An attic fan that's too powerful is not a problem— it simply will shut itself off when the attic is cool—but a fan without sufficient power will grind away for hours and wear out quickly.

CONTROLS: Because an attic is seldom easily accessible, most attic fans have thermostats so they turn on when needed and shut off when the attic is cool.

If your area has humid summers, buy a fan that also has a humidistat so it will switch on to draw out moist air even when the temperature is not high. Removing moisture not only keeps the house more comfortable, but also protects insulation and wood from moisture damage.

You may want to install an override switch so you can turn off the fan at summer's end or when the house will be vacant.

INSTALLING A FAN

If possible, install a gable-mounted attic fan so you can avoid the time-consuming task of installing a roof jack. Cut a hole for the fan and mount it on the inside with screws. Install a louvered panel on the outside if the area is subject to rain or snow. Most homes, however, require a roof vent.

CUT THE HOLE: To install a fan on the roof, drill a small hole centered between two joists, near the top of the roof. Push a piece of wire through the hole so you can see it easily when you're on the roof.

Using the hole as a reference point, set the fan on top of the roof and slide it up under a row of shingles; the hole does not have to be in the exact center. Trace the outline of the fan flashing on the roofing.

The fan will come with a template for making a circular cutout of the shingles. Cut the circle with a utility knife—it will

Rafter

1. Drill a reference hole near the top of the roof between two joists. Drill through the sheathing and out through the roofing. Poke a piece of wire out through the hole so you can find it when you are on the roof.

2. Determine the best position for the fan so it can slip up under as many shingles as possible. Use templates to cut out a circle of shingles and then to cut out the sheathing.

Shingle cutout is larger than hole in sheathing

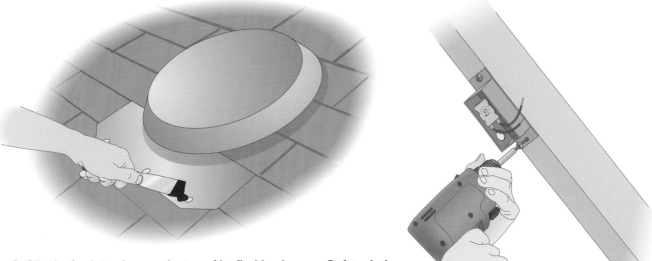

3. *Slip the fan into place so the top of its flashing is covered with shingles and the bottom of its flashing rests on top of shingles. Seal the underside of the flashing with roofing cement, drive nails, and seal the nail heads with roofing cement.*

4. *Attach the thermostat to a joist. Be sure to locate it away from the air flow caused by the fan.*

take several passes—and remove the shingles inside the circle.

Cut a smaller hole through the plywood or 1-by sheathing, using a saber saw or a reciprocating saw.

ATTACH THE FAN: Slide the fan flashing up under as many shingles as possible. Shingles should cover the top two-thirds of the flashing; the bottom third of the flashing should cover shingles. Slip roofing cement under the flashing, attach with a few nails, and cover the nail heads with dollops of roofing cement.

MAKE ELECTRICAL CONNECTIONS: Attach the thermostat to a nearby joist. Shut off power to the circuit. Run 2-wire cable to a junction box. Run three-wire cable from the junction box to the thermostat, and from the junction box to a switch box on the top floor of the house.

At the switch box, connect all three wires to the switch.

At the junction box, connect the hot wire to the black wire leading to the switch. Connect the red wires together. Connect the white wire from the power source to the white wire going to the thermostat, and connect the black wire going to the thermostat with the white wire going to the switch. At the thermostat, make connections as shown (*right*).

ADJUST THE THERMOSTAT: Restore power and test the fan. Use a screwdriver to adjust the thermostat's temperature setting.

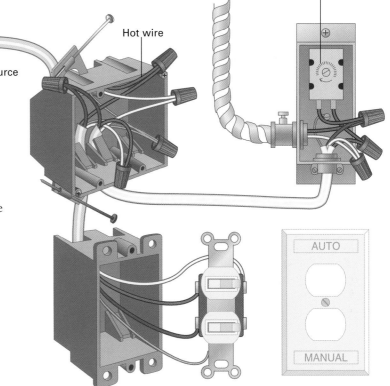

Power source

Hot wire

Thermostat

AUTO

MANUAL

5. *Run cable and make electrical connections as shown. Or, bring power to the switch box first, and then to the thermostat. See manufacturer's instructions for specific wiring directions.*

BACK-TO-BACK OUTDOOR BOX

Often, an outdoor receptacle can tie into an interior receptacle. Install a GFCI receptacle with a weatherproof cover near, but not directly behind, an interior receptacle.

Usually an outdoor receptacle does not have to be precisely located, so choose the most convenient method of installation. Put the outside box near—but not directly opposite—an existing interior receptacle. If you need to place the receptacle elsewhere, see page 60 for instructions on using fish tape.

Choose an interior receptacle in a box that has room for more wires; an end-of-the-run receptacle with only two wires is ideal. Check that its circuit will not be overloaded by the new receptacle (*see pages 70–71*).

DRILL THROUGH TO THE OUTSIDE: Shut off the power and test for power in the receptacle box. Pull the interior receptacle out of the box.

Use a long ¼-inch drill bit to bore a hole through the back of the box all the way out through the exterior of the house. (If the box is metal with knockout holes in the back, punch one out first. For a plastic box, just drill through.) If your house exterior is masonry, use a masonry bit. In either case, angle the drill bit so the hole does not end up directly opposite the interior box.

CUT A HOLE: With your drilled hole as a reference point on the exterior of the house, use a box for a template, and cut out a hole for it (*see pages 62–63*). For wood siding, drill a hole large enough for a blade to fit in, and cut with a saber saw or keyhole saw. On a masonry wall, drill a series of holes with a masonry bit around the perimeter of your outline, and chip out the interior of the hole with a hammer and cold chisel.

RUN CABLE: Strip sheathing from a piece of cable, and attach a cable clamp to it. Reach through the exterior hole and push the cable through the interior box. If possible, have someone hold the cable in position while you go indoors and screw on the clamp nut to hold the cable in place.

Outside, strip the sheathing from the other end of the cable, and clamp it in the new box. Install the box. If your exterior wall is masonry, drive screws through the back of the box into a stud, or pack mortar around the box.

INSTALL THE EXTERIOR RECEPTACLE: Purchase a GFCI receptacle with a weatherproof cover. Wire the receptacle (*see page 37*) and screw it to the box. Add the foam insulation and the hinged cover plate.

Replace the interior receptacle, restore power, and test.

Existing receptacle

Stud

New GFCI receptacle

Weatherproof gasket and cover

PERMANENT OUTDOOR FIXTURES

I f low-voltage lighting (*see page 51*) is not strong enough, or if you need to install a receptacle away from the house, check with local codes to find out how to run outdoor cable in your area. Some localities allow UF cable (*see page 20*) installed directly in the ground; others require that UF cable be run through plastic or metal conduit. The conduit is not expensive and provides protection against shovels. Also find out which boxes are approved for outdoor use, and how deep the trenches must be.

EXCAVATE: If you have a long way to go, rent a trench digger. Not only will it save you the effort of digging, but it will make it easier to replace the sod. To run cable underneath a sidewalk, dig a trench on each side. Use a hammer to drive a piece of metal pipe under the concrete. Remove the pipe carefully so the hole remains, and tap in a length of conduit.

PROVIDE POSTS: Wherever you want a light or an exterior receptacle, solidly anchor a post if there is not one there already. Use a post-hole digger to dig a hole at least 2 feet deep. Set a pressure-treated 4×4 post in the hole, slightly below grade for a lamp, or a couple of feet above grade for a receptacle. Check the post to see that it is plumb. Pour concrete in the hole, tamp it firm, and allow it to set.

INSTALL BOXES AND DEVICES: For lighting, you may want to install a switch inside the house. Exterior lights can be controlled with a motion sensor or with a photovoltaic switch that turns them on when it gets dark.

Shut off power to the circuit before connecting to a junction box. Use a switch and a GFCI receptacle enclosed in a weathertight box. Exterior boxes are made of aluminum or a rust-proof metal alloy. The holes and the conduit are threaded. The boxes come with plugs to seal any holes not being used by conduit. Caulk threads prior to sealing holes for a watertight seal.

Mount the boxes using rust-proof all-purpose screws. Clamp the conduit or UF cable within 8 inches of the box. Strip sheathing and wire ends and connect to terminals as you would for interior devices (*see pages 25–27*). Install a foam gasket and cover with spring-loaded doors to protect the receptacles and switches from weather when they are not in use. Restore power, and test. Fill in the trench, taking care not to place sharp rocks up against the cable or conduit.

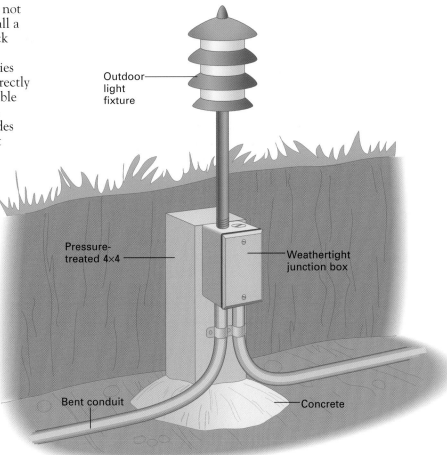

Outdoor light fixture

Pressure-treated 4×4

Weathertight junction box

Bent conduit

Concrete

For a permanent outdoor light fixture, fasten it to a pressure-treated 4×4 set in concrete and run conduit to it.

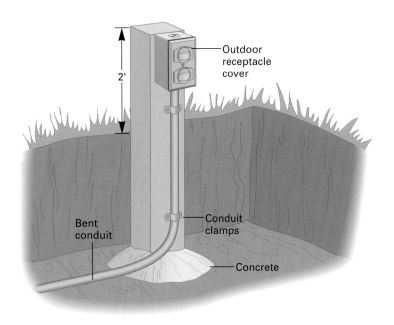

Outdoor receptacle cover

2'

Bent conduit

Conduit clamps

Concrete

When you are unable to attach an outdoor receptacle to a building, install a post at least 2 feet above grade for a receptacle in an exposed position.

INDEX

A

Additions, new service for, 71
Air conditioners
  power use by, 52
  thermostats for, 49
Amps
  circuit capacity and, 12
  defined, 10
  switches and, 23
  wire size and, 20
Appliances
  amp ratings for, 10, 12
  circuits for, 10–11, 52–53
  receptacles for, 78
Armored (BX) cable
  boxes for, 21
  described, 20
  safety with, 17
  working with, 52, 54–55
Attics
  fans in, 90–91
  running cable through, 60–61

B

Ballasts, 43
Baseboards
  raceway, 69
  running cable behind, 68
Basements
  circuits for, 12, 70
  running cables through, 61
Bathrooms
  circuits for, 12, 70
  vent fans for, 88
Box extenders, 37
Boxes
  connecting cable to, 55, 59
  in finished ceilings, 64–65
  in finished walls, 62–63
  outdoor, 92–93
  plastic, 17, 21
  safety with, 16–17
  types of, 21
  in unfinished walls, 58
  weight of ceiling fixtures and,
      41, 44
Breaker boxes
  adding new circuits to, 72–73
  described, 8–9
  marking, 4, 12
  resetting, 8–9
Brick lighting, 51
Building codes
  adding circuits and, 70–71
  adhering to, 5–6, 11
  for outdoor cable, 93
  for raceway wiring, 69
  for receptacle placement, 58
Bus bars, in service panel, 8

Bushings, for armored cable, 17, 55
BX cable. See Armored cable
BX cutter, 54

C

Cable clamps, 17
Cable rippers, 25
Cable TV wiring, 74–75
Cables. See also Wires; specific types
  in attics, 60–61
  in basements, 61
  in finished spaces, 66–68
  safety with, 15, 17
  types of, 20, 51, 74–75
  in unfinished spaces, 58–59
Canister lights, recessed
  choosing, 86
  installing, 87
Carpeting, hiding cable under, 75
Ceiling boxes
  attaching cable to, 59
  braced, 64–65
  described, 21
  in finished ceilings, 64–65
  placement of, 58
  weight of fixtures and, 41, 44
Ceiling fans
  boxes for, 21, 41, 44
  braced box, 44
  clearances for, 45
  grounding, 64
  installing, 45
Ceiling fixtures. See also specific types
  adding new, 68
  replacing, 41
  wiring for, 79
Chandeliers, boxes for, 41
Chimes. See Doorbells and chimes
Circuit breakers
  adding new, 72–73
  described, 8, 38
  GFCI, 37–39
  replacing, 38–39
  resetting, 8–9, 38–39
  safety with, 38
  skinnies, 38, 72
Circuits
  adding new, 72–73
  evaluating, 12, 71
  mapping, 4, 12
  overloaded, 8, 11–12, 52, 71
  planning new, 70–71
  shutting off, 6
  types of, 10–11, 52–53
Color coding, on wire insulation, 20
Common terminal, explained, 82
Computers, surge protection for, 40
Conduit
  boxes for, 21
  described, 20, 56

  plastic, 20
  pulling wires through, 57
  running, 57
Conduit benders, 56–57
Connectors, for conduit, 56
Continuity testers
  described, 19
  using, 35
Cords
  extension, 12, 30
  replacing, 30
  safety with, 14
Couplings, for conduit, 56

D

Dimmer switches
  described, 22
  three-way, 36, 84
  wiring for, 36
Disconnect, main, 8, 72–73
Doorbells and chimes
  repairing, 46–48
  wireless, 48
Double switches
  described, 22
  wiring for, 36
Double-pole switches, 35
Drills/drilling, 58–61
Dryers, power use by, 52
Drywall saws, 18–19
Ductwork, for vent fan, 88

E

Electric meters, reading, 9
Electrical metal tubing (EMT), 56
Electricity, path of, 7
Electrocution, 78
EMT, 56
Extension cords, 12, 30

F

Fans
  attic, 90–91
  bathroom vent, 88
  ceiling, 41, 44–45, 64
  whole-house, 89
Feed-through switches, 31
Fire hazards, 14, 17
Fish tape, 18–19, 60
Flexible conduit, 56
Fluorescent lighting, 43
Four-way switches
  described, 22
  wiring for, 85
Framing, rough electric in, 58–59
Fuse boxes
  described, 9
  new circuits and, 72
  replacing fuses in, 39
  safety with, 38
Fuse puller, 39

G

Garages, circuits for, 12, 70
General-purpose circuits, 10
GFCI
  circuit breakers, 37–39
  receptacles, 24, 37, 92–93
GRC, 56
Greenfield, 53, 56
Ground Fault Circuit Interrupter.
  See GFCI
Grounding
  main, 8, 13
  plugs, 30
  receptacles, 13, 32–33
  switches, 22
Guard strips, 59, 66

H

Hacksaw, cutting armored cable
    with, 55
Halogen lights, under-cabinet, 50
Handy boxes, 21
Heating units, thermostats for, 49
High voltage, safety and, 78

I

IMC, 56
Individual circuits, 10–11
In-line switches, 31
Insulation, wire
  color coding of, 20
  damaged, 17
  types of, 20
Intermediate conduit (IMC), 56

J

Joists, cutting, 87
Jumper wires, 46, 49
Junction boxes, 21

K

Kitchens, circuits for, 10, 12, 52–53, 70
Knockouts, 72

L

Lamps
  switches, 31
  wiring in, 28–29
Laundries, circuits for, 12, 70
Light bulbs
  as fire hazards, 14
  flood, 86
  fluorescent, 43
  incandescent, 31
Light fixtures
  ceiling, 41, 68, 79
  circuits for, 12, 15
  as fire hazards, 14
  fluorescent, 43
  outdoor, 51, 93
  recessed canister, 86–87

switch configurations for, 79–85
  track, 42
  under-cabinet halogen, 50
  wall sconces, 76–77
Lineman's pliers, 18–19, 26
Living areas, circuits for, 70

M

Main disconnect, 8, 72–73
Moldings, running cable behind, 66,
    75
Motion-sensor security switches
  described, 23
  wiring for, 36
Multi-testers, 6, 48

N

National Electrical Code (NEC),
    5, 6, 11
Neon testers
  circuit testing with, 6
  described, 19
  doorbell testing with, 47–48
  receptacle testing with, 32–33
  switch testing with, 31, 35
New construction, wiring in, 58–59
Nonmetallic (NM) cable
  boxes for, 21
  described, 20
  stripping, 25
  vs. armored, 54
  working with, 52

O

Outdoor lighting
  low-voltage, 51
  permanent, 93
Outlet boxes, 21
Outlets, defined, 9
Overhead service, 7
Overloads
  avoiding, 11
  breaker or fuse size and, 8
  circuit capacity and, 12, 71
  new service and, 52, 71

P–Q

Paneling, installing boxes in, 63
Pen-type mini-voltmeter, 32
Phone lines. *See* Telephone lines
Pigtails, 16, 34
Pilot-light switches, 23
Plaster, installing boxes in, 62–63, 65
Plastic (PVC) conduit, 56
Plugs
  replacing, 30
  safety with, 14
Polarization, 13, 30
Power companies, service from, 7
Programmable switches, 23
Programmable thermostats, 49

Pulling elbow, 57
PVC conduit, 56
Quick-connect plugs, 30

R

Raceway wiring, 69
Receptacle analyzers
  described, 19
  using, 13, 32
Receptacles
  adding new, 78
  connection holes in, 27
  defined, 9
  GFCI, 24, 37, 92–93
  grounded, 13, 32–33
  height of, 58, 62
  number needed, 12
  outdoor, 92–93
  polarized, 13
  replacing, 33
  safety with, 14, 16
  surge-protecting, 40
  switch-controlled, 10, 24, 34
  testing, 6, 10, 12, 32–33
  250-volt, 78
  types of, 24, 37
  wiring for, 34, 78, 92
Reciprocating saws, 19
Refrigerators, power use by, 52
Remodeling, wiring in, 52, 71
Rigid conduit (GRC), 56
Rocker switches, 22–23
Rough electric, 58–59

S

Safety
  in electrical systems, 13, 15–17
  in electrical work, 6, 8, 38, 78
  in the home, 14
Saws
  drywall, 18–19
  hacksaw, 55
  reciprocating, 19
Service panels
  adding circuits to, 72–73
  capacity of, 15, 71
  knockouts in, 72
  operation of, 8
  shutting off service to, 8, 72–73
  types of, 8–9
Service wires, 6–8
Single-pole switches, 22
Skinnies, 38, 72
Small-appliance circuits, 10
Speaker wire, 20, 30
Splices, 15, 26
Staples, insulated, 59
Static electricity, 40
Stud finder, electronic, 60
Studs, notching, 58, 66–67
Surface-mounted wiring, 69

Surge protection, 40
Switch boxes, 21
Switches, wall. *See also* Lamps, switches
  basic, 22–23
  connection holes in, 27
  height of, 58
  replacing, 35
  safety with, 16
  special-use, 22–23, 36
  testing, 35
  wiring for, 79–85
Switch-receptacles, 10, 24, 34

T

Telephone lines
  surge protection for, 40
  wiring, 74–75
Television, wiring for cable service, 74–75
Testers, voltage, 6
  meter, 19
  neon, 19
  pen-type, 32
Terminal connections, 16, 27
Thermostats
  attic fan, 90
  heating or cooling, 49
Thin-wall conduit, 56
Three-way switches
  described, 22
  dimmers, 36, 84
  with receptacle, 85
  testing, 35
  wiring for, 82–84

Timer switches, 23
Tools. *See also specific tools*
  basic, 18–19
  safe, 6
Track lighting, 42
Transformers
  doorbell, 46–48
  halogen light, 50
  outdoor light, 51
  power company, 7
  thermostat, 49
Tubing cutter, 57
250-volt receptacles, 24, 78

U

UF cable. *See* Underground feeder cable
UL symbols, 23
Underground feeder (UF) cable, 20
Underground service, 7
Underwriter's knot, 30
Underwriters Laboratory (UL) symbols, 23
Utility areas, circuits for, 12, 70
Utility boxes, 21

V

Vent fans, bathroom, 88
Voltage ratings, changes in, 7
Voltage testers, 6
Volt/amp meter
  described, 19
  doorbell testing with, 46–47
  receptacle testing with, 32–33
  switch testing with, 35

Volts
  circuit capacity and, 12
  defined, 10

W

Wall sconces, 76–77
Wallboard, installing boxes in, 62–65
Waterproof cable, 20
Watts
  circuit capacity and, 12
  defined, 10
Whole-house fans, 89
Wire nuts, 15, 26
Wire strippers, 18–19
Wires. *See also* Cables
  connecting to terminals, 16, 27
  matching receptacles to, 24
  pulling through conduit, 57
  safety with, 15–16
  specifications of, 20
  splicing, 15, 26
  stripping, 16, 25
Wiring configurations
  canister lights, 87
  fans, 88–91
  receptacles, 34, 78
  switches, 79–85
Wiring runs
  doorbell, testing, 48
  GFCI, 37
  "home run," 72
  receptacle, 34
  roughing-in, 58–59
  surface-mounted, 69
Workshops, circuits for, 12, 70

METRIC CONVERSIONS

U.S. Units to Metric Equivalents			Metric Units to U.S. Equivalents		
To Convert From	Multiply By	To Get	To Convert From	Multiply By	To Get
Inches	25.4	Millimeters	Millimeters	0.0394	Inches
Inches	2.54	Centimeters	Centimeters	0.3937	Inches
Feet	30.48	Centimeters	Centimeters	0.0328	Feet
Feet	0.3048	Meters	Meters	3.2808	Feet
Yards	0.9144	Meters	Meters	1.0936	Yards
Square inches	6.4516	Square centimeters	Square centimeters	0.1550	Square inches
Square feet	0.0929	Square meters	Square meters	10.764	Square feet
Square yards	0.8361	Square meters	Square meters	1.1960	Square yards
Acres	0.4047	Hectares	Hectares	2.4711	Acres
Cubic inches	16.387	Cubic centimeters	Cubic centimeters	0.0610	Cubic inches
Cubic feet	0.0283	Cubic meters	Cubic meters	35.315	Cubic feet
Cubic feet	28.316	Liters	Liters	0.0353	Cubic feet
Cubic yards	0.7646	Cubic meters	Cubic meters	1.308	Cubic yards
Cubic yards	764.55	Liters	Liters	0.0013	Cubic yards

To convert from degrees Fahrenheit (F) to degrees Celsius (C), first subtract 32, then multiply by 5/9.

To convert from degrees Celsius to degrees Fahrenheit, multiply by 9/5, then add 32.